How We Raised
A Hyperactive Child
and
Lived To Tell About It
and
<u>YOU</u> Can Too!!!

In Richard and Johnie
Beverly Lowry

By
Beverly D. Lowry

How We Raised A
Hyperactive Child
and
Lived To Tell About It
and
YOU Can Too!!

Beverly D. Lowry
© 2009

ISBN : 978-0-9788835-0-8

SAN Number = 851-8688

LL&L, Inc.
3937 Fort Avenue
Lynchburg, VA 24502

Dedication

Having lived the experience of participating in the short seventeen years of raising a "Creative" son, I felt I had the need to write this book.

I have tried to give hope to all the Mothers, Fathers, and other family members of a "Hyper-Creative" child.

Without the main person of this story, I would not have had a story to tell, nor would I feel as though I had any right to write such a book. Therefore, I dedicate this book to my son, Mark!

I asked Mark to write any remarks he would like to add to any portion of this book, and they are his remarks, completely unedited.

Your Dad and I thank GOD for allowing us the privilege of raising you, Mark.

We love you Mark, and your brother, Mike, and sister, Melissa. We are thankful that GOD showed us through our children how to help others.

You are a blessing.

Love,

Mama

Table of Contents

Introduction

QUESTION: Why this book?

ANSWER: Traveling around the United States and Canada for several years speaking at Christian Women's Conferences, I have been asked hundreds of time, "How did you raise Mark?"

I taught Child Psychology at Liberty University for seventeen years and retired in 2003. In 2004 I became an adjunct professor and have had the pleasure of not only teaching at Liberty University, but also speaking at Christian Women's Conferences and Mother-Daughter Banquets in the United States and Canada and I have met many Mothers, aunts, uncles and siblings of hyperactive children, who are seeking help concerning a hyperactive child.

I asked my husband, Charles, to help me put in writing the story of how we raised our hyperactive son, Mark.

I will tell you about our lives, and how we held onto God's promises. God is and has been our strength, help, and best Friend. He will be yours also.

I will tell you up front that we were not perfect parents, nor will I tell you we raised a perfect hyperactive child. However, I will tell you of our daily struggles, joys and triumphs, not only with our hyperactive child, but also about some of the characters we encountered along the way.

I feel that the major one who God used to accomplish this was Charles. I learned many years later that God put children as babies in a home for the reason of getting a concept of who God is. The Father shows the discipline and sovereignty of God to a child. The Mother shows the unconditional love of God.

It is very difficult for one parent to show both of the concepts of God and Charles did a great job of discipline. (For whom the LORD loveth he correcteth; even as a father the son in whom he delighteth. Proverbs 3:12) (Correct thy son, and he shall give thee rest; yea, he shall give delight unto thy soul. Proverbs 29:13). All Scripture verses in this book are King James version.

This is the way God intended a family to be. But, even with God's blessing, we all make mistakes. There are no perfect parents. We would be the first to admit that we made mistakes. If we could live our lives over, there are definitely some things we would do differently and I hope to point out our mistakes and help young parents to benefit by our good experiences and mistakes.

We believe that God has taught us much in His word about raising a family and also through much prayer He gives us the strength to do what He said. Again, I am not saying we did a perfect job or that our children are perfect, however, I am happy to report that all three of our children love God and are actively working for Him.

This book is written mainly because so many people have asked me how we dealt with a hyperactive child.

We did not have a Mark Lowry going around the country talking about hyperactivity when we were raising Mark, but we did have our faith in our Heavenly Father and we stayed in touch with Him on a daily basis through our Lord and Savior and Advocate, Jesus Christ.

And, Yes, a Hyperactive Child will keep you prayed up!!!

Mark's Remarks

Gloria Gaither put together a book several years ago entitled, *What My Parents Did Right.* I wrote a chapter in it. I don't own the book, I'm 50 years old and my memory doesn't serve me well, but I think I said, the thing they did right was they believed in me.

I still think that is one of the things they did right. My parents always encouraged me to succeed. If I sang, they thought it was Shakespeare. Yes, they believed in me, to a fault. I can't trust them to tell me what I *need* to hear when I write a lyric. Because they, like me, think my ugly children are as wonderful as my beautiful kids. (My lyrics are my kids.)

I was telling a friend today that one of the things my parents did right was the assurance I had of their love for *each other.* I've never gone to bed worried that they might not love each other in the morning. And the thought never crossed my mind that they could ever stop loving me. As I've said somewhere in some other book before, people couldn't chop down enough trees and make enough paper and write enough notes and pin them to my lapel (reminding me and telling my parents all the bad things I'd done in school) to cause my parents to stop loving me.

And after much protest (from me) my mother is writing a book...about me. I told her, "Don't make me a trophy, I'm not done yet! And, if your're gonna write this book, we're gonna tell it all. We're gonna show our scars or I'll have no part of it. Nobody helps anybody by showing somebody their trophy. But, if they show their scars they can help everybody."

And, I told her, "I want the last word in every chapter."

She sweetly submitted. It was the first time.

Okay, okay, it was the first time she ever submitted…to me.

God has no standards, He can use anybody. Just look at the two He chose to raise His Son? A 13-year-old girl and a man we know little about. They weren't perfect parents by a long shot. Have you ever lost one of your kids for two days BEFORE you thought to look for him?

Well, they did. They were two days into their journey home from Jerusalem when it dawned on them to look for Jesus! And you thought you were a lousy parent because you lost your kid at Wal Mart for twenty minutes. Listen! God can use anybody!

When Mom started traveling around the world (US and CANADA, but when your're in your 70's that's world enough) speaking in conferences, I asked her if she had anything to say to the single parents. She says in the introduction: "the father gives the discipline and the mother gives the love."

I say, "Blah, blah, blah, blah."

I got both from both. I was loved by them both and I got my rear-end torn up by both. Unfortunately, there are many single parents who must give both the discipline and the love. It can be done. Of course, it's easier with two parents. But even then it's not a perfect scenario, at best it's broken, because we live in a broken world. We can only do our best. And my mom and dad did their best. But, it wasn't, The Cleavers. Who, by the way, are the original dysfunctional family. I never saw mom wearing pearls while doing laundry. And I bet you didn't either.

Yes, it's easier with two parents, but it can be done by one. It can be done by anyone who knows how to love, guide and direct a child.

Oh, by the way, I have no psych degree and no kids. But, I'm right.

Take it away, Mama…

The Hyper-Creative one.

Developmental Stages of a Boy

As everyone knows there are several stages of development of a child from infancy to adulthood. Charles came up with these stages and I asked him to share them here.

The following revelation is from observing the development of two younger brothers, cousins, nephews and my own two sons, from infancy to adulthood.

After birth to approximately three years of age he is a Mother's boy.

Around three years of age, he has figured out that many good things can be obtained from Daddy, so he becomes a Daddy's boy and remains so until around seven years of age.

At seven years of age he has learned how to play Mother against Daddy to get what he wants.

At ten years of age he starts asking for a horse and this will continue until he is fourteen. (Especially if he is raised in Texas).

At fourteen years of age:

1. He is usually as tall or taller than his Mother and resents any woman telling him what to do.

    Note to all Mothers: At this stage, when it becomes necessary for the mother to correct/scold her son, she should have him sit in a chair, and stand in front of him with her finger pointing down toward him when she gives him some type of correction. Pointing your finger down toward someone has a lot more authority than pointing your finger up toward someone. This is the very reason a judge in a courtroom sits higher than anyone else. You look up to authority.

2. He has hormones running amuck in his body.

3. Pimples (Zits) start showing up on his face.

4. He has discovered girls.

5. He is finally taller than most girls in his classroom.

6. He is active in some form of sports or has taken an interest in some activity that takes his time away from his parents.

7. He spends a lot of time combing and grooming his hair.

8. Girls have started calling him on the telephone. (Nice girls do not call boys).

9. He has become a loner and does not want to be bothered by his younger siblings.

10. He spends a lot of time on computer type games.

At fifteen, he is enrolled in Driver's Education and after obtaining his permit to drive with a licensed driver in the front seat, he gets behind the steering wheel every time any licensed family member gets in the family car.

At sixteen, he starts driving and feels he has stepped into a new dimension, and he has.

At seventeen he starts thinking about his future, such as college.

Also, at eighteen he advises his parents they have been good parents as he prepares to enter college.

At eighteen he enters college and once again he is on the lower end of the status poll. Seniors are at the top.

Four years of college is four years of maturing and then after graduation he starts full time employment and eventually moves out of the family home.

At some point in time, he meets the most beautiful girl and they marry and live Happily Ever-After!

After marriage, he decides that Mother and Daddy have really learned a lot between his seventeenth birthday and his twenty-fifth birthday.

He then starts a mature relationship with his Mother and Dad.

Now you know the Developmental Stages of a Boy.

Chapter One
Making The Mark
(The Story Begins)

On the beautiful morning of June twenty-four
The stork laid a bundle at our front door.
Mark Alan Lowry will be his name,
We're so very glad that to us he came.
He tips the scales at eight pounds, 14 1/2 ounces.
And just like his brother, he's so round he bounces.
He looks a lot like daddy and also big brother,
And we wouldn't trade him for any other.
We now number four at Victoria Drive,
And who knows but someday we may number five.
But for now we've two apples to highlight our eyes
And our hearts are still soaring clear up to the skies.
—Charles and Beverly Lowry, 1958

And that is exactly how we felt on that morning, June 24, 1958. We had two little boys that were very much wanted and loved.

Mark was a special little boy even before he was born—I had planned to have two children, two years apart. So in June of 1957 Charles and I began a pregnancy that we hoped would be our second child.

On August 1st, two months into the pregnancy, I miscarried. Oh how I grieved over that baby. I wanted that child.

I suppose that this was normal, but if I could only have trusted God more I would have realized that He knows best and is working all things for my good.

I began another pregnancy on October 1, 1957. Two months into that pregnancy, on December 1st, I took Mike downtown to have his second year picture made for his birthday that would be on December 3rd.

I carried Mike, of course. When I got back to my Mother's house my water broke. I thought I would miscarry for the second time.

I was put to bed and remained there for three weeks. Dr. Paton said, "Mrs. Lowry, if the tear is high in the uterus the tear will mend and the water will replenish. If the tear is low in the uterus the water will continue to seep out and you will miscarry this baby."

During that time in bed I became very despondent. My two-year-old child had to be cared for. My house had to be cared for and I was laid up in bed. I began to have headaches from lying in bed so long.

Reading my Bible was the best comfort that I could have and one day I picked up my Bible and turned to Psalm 27. It is still my favorite Psalm in the Bible.

"V.1 The Lord is my light and my salvation; whom shall I fear? The Lord is the strength of my life; of whom shall I be afraid?

v. 4 One thing have I desired of the Lord, that will I seek after; that I may dwell in the house of the Lord all the days of my life, to behold the beauty of the Lord, and to inquire in his temple.

v. 5 For in the time of trouble he shall hide me in his pavilion: in the secret of his tabernacle shall he hide me; he shall set me up upon a rock. (Jesus). The Psalmist goes on to ask the Lord to lead him in a Plain Path.

v. 14 Wait on the Lord: be of good courage and he shall strengthen thine heart: wait, I say, on the Lord."

The Lord had spoken to me in a very real way. I asked the Lord to please let me have his baby. "Lord," I said, 'If You will let me have this baby, You can have 'her' in Your service even if it's on a mission field someday." For me the ultimate sacrifice for a parent was to let their child go to the mission field. Mark is on a mission field today. It would be years later that the Lord would remind me of that conversation. And "her" turned out to be a "him. "

My neighbor, Helen Eaton, came every morning and took Mike home with her. At noon she brought me a sandwich. Thank God for neighbors who love God and are willing to help in a crisis.

After three weeks the doctor told me to come to his office and let him check me over. After this checkup he told me to get out of bed. He thought the crisis was over. The water was replenishing and the baby was fine.

On June 24, 1958, I delivered a healthy 8 lb. 14 1/2 oz. baby boy. He was beautiful and really had good lungs. He still does.

The first year of Mark's life was relatively calm. He loved people that he knew and disliked strangers.

When he began walking, he began running. He wasn't mean. He just liked to have fun. Things that seemed like fun to him really bothered others. By the time he turned two he had become anything but calm. When Mike set up a line of toy soldiers to play with, Mark thought that really he had set them up for him to come in and kick them as far as he could. Real war would break out.

Mark didn't enjoy sitting and playing anything in a quiet manner. His idea of fun was to run and kick, and in his mind that was having a good time.

His dislike for strangers changed. By the time he was four he could hold a conversation with any stranger he met. When we went to a restaurant to eat he would eat as quickly as possible and then he would ask if he could go up to the cashier to talk with her and we told him, "Yes, but don't leave the area." As we paid our check and left she would say, "Bye Mark, see you next time." In the car Mark would tell us how many children she had, her marital status, how much her rings cost, whether or not she went to Church and where, also where her children went to school. He loved to talk to strangers and they seemed to like talking with him.

He loved old people and babies, and he still does.

He wasn't a smart aleck. But he thought that he knew as much about what we were talking about as we did.

Mike, age 4, Mama, Mark, age 2

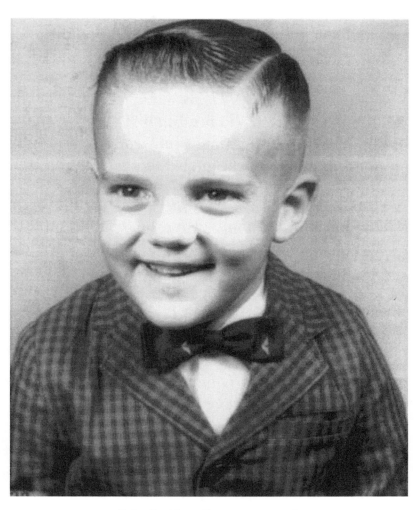

Mark Alan Lowry, age 2

Chapter Two
Marking Time
(Elementary School)

I took a piece of plastic clay
And idly fashioned it one day.
And as my fingers pressed it still,
It moved and yielded to my will.
I came again when days were past.
The bit of clay was hard at last
The form I gave it, it still bore
But I could change that form no more.
I took a piece of living clay
And gently formed it day by day,
And molded with my power and art
A young child's soft and yielding heart.
I came again when years were gone,
It was a man I looked upon
He still that early impress wore-
And I could change him never more.
—Author Unknown

Walking out of the principal's office, I felt a heavy burden. What was happening to Mark? Was he just a robust, over-active little boy? Or was there really something wrong with him? Was he any different than the other little boys? Questions whirled around in my head.

Mark had been one of the younger ones in his class at the beginning of school. His birthday was June 24, 1958, so he turned five in the summer and began kindergarten in the fall. The children whose birthday was in September, October, November and December had turned five almost a year before him. If I had that to do over again I would let him wait a year to begin school so that he would be one of the older ones in his class. It would have given him a little more maturity and I know now that it would have given him more social and cognitive development.

I can remember the day that I left him in kindergarten. It took two teachers to hold him and he was kicking and fighting to get free. He wanted to go home with me. By the end of the week he had calmed down. He told my mother, however, on the phone that week, "Nanny, I knew it was going to get hard, and it did."

In the first and second grade, I didn't get notes from the teachers, I got four page letters. Many a night I went to bed crying and praying, "Lord, help me to understand and give me wisdom to help him."

He never seemed to have any trouble in doing the schoolwork assigned to him, and in the fall of 1966 he entered the third grade and was put in the accelerated class with a young teacher, Miss Johnson. This was her first year out of college. This class was for the students who could do better and more advanced work.

She expected her accelerated students to sit with hands folded and listen to her lecture. This would be a hard task for any group of third graders. For Mark it was impossible.

In school, he did not want to sit down and be quiet like the teachers wanted him to. He wanted to get up when he felt like it. He wanted to run around the room.

About two weeks into the semester she caught him running in the cafeteria and put him behind a partition, separated from the rest of the class. Now I can understand her getting after him for running; however, I had seen many children running in the cafeteria. I could also understand the "time out" from the rest of the class. But she placed him behind a partition in her classroom for three weeks.

One night at a PTA meeting Miss Johnson told me that Mark was walking in from the playground and he made his mouth look deformed.

He said, "It's O.K., Miss Johnson, I was born this way."

She thought that he was awful for saying that. I knew that he only wanted to make her laugh.

At that moment I felt that Mark was not the total problem here. I knew that he was trying, in his own way, to win her over. He felt that if he could make her laugh she might like him. I really felt that he was fighting a losing battle. She had read the remarks in the permanent record made by the other teachers and had made up her mind that Mark really was a problem and that he would never change. I feel that it is wrong for teachers to read permanent records until the end of the first semester. Children should be able to make their own record each year. Maybe during the summer they changed. Maybe they had a life changing experience. But teachers tend to push them back into the same mold. It is really hard for anyone to change if everyone expects them to act a certain way. It becomes a self-fulfilling prophecy.

Mark used to come home from her class with four page letters pinned to his shirt. A simple note wasn't enough. The agony that this caused all of us was unbearable. I didn't know how to handle this at all. I was only thirty-two at the time and this was something that I did not understand. After all, the teacher is supposed to be the professional. As a young Mother I was trusting the system to help Mark, not hurt him.

I called my pediatrician, Dr. Stool, and told him all about it. He said, "He is smarter than the teacher. He is wanting her to like him and he thinks that she will, if he can get her to smile at him. Home should be a refuge. She should handle problems at school and not expect you to handle them at home."

He told me to call the school and request a psychometric evaluation of Mark to see if he was placed in the right class. Miss Johnson's class was accelerated, which meant that these children had a higher IQ than the average class.

When I asked the principal, Mrs. Wilkerson, to get Mark evaluated, she was delighted. She moved him to the top of the long list of children waiting for the exam and made the appointment with the psychologist for the next week.

I told Mark that he had been chosen to take the tests. I felt that he needed something to make him feel special and I didn't want him to feel that it had anything to do with his conduct.

After that test, the psychologist told me that Mark was above average in intelligence. But that he had a low frustration level. She really didn't mention hyperactivity to me. At that time there was no test to determine hyperactivity.

If a child was more active than other children, we just considered him to be bad. Sometimes they gave Ritalin to a child. Ritalin would speed up adults, but it slowed a child down. The pediatrician did give Ritalin to Mark, and on the third day, I passed his classroom and saw him asleep, with his head on his desk. So I stopped it. I felt that he needed to be awake in class and not drugged.

When the psychologist examined him, she said she really could not put a number on his IQ, but she knew it was high because if she gave him a hard problem to do, he would do it. Then she would give him another problem along the same lines that was easy and he would just say he couldn't do it.

She said that he needed a firm hand in front that said, "STOP" and at the same time he needed a hand patting him on the back saying, "That's good."

Although he could do the work, she didn't feel that he should be required to work at top level all the time, and that he needed to be out of the accelerated class.

She told me that Mark had a lot to say about his older brother. He felt that Mike was perfect, he could play football, and Daddy had taught him how to box and things like that.

She asked me if my husband and I would come in for another set of tests and she definitely wanted Daddy to come in with him. We did.

She told my husband that Mark felt that his Daddy was partial to Mike. He felt that Daddy worked with Mike more on things that Mike liked to do.

Charles made a 180-degree turn. He made sure that he included Mark in all of the things he did with Mike.

A lot of Fathers might have trouble being told by a psychologist that they are doing something wrong, but Charles is a very intelligent man and he and I loved Mark equally as much as we loved Mike.

He realized that it really didn't matter what we thought. What Mark thought was what really counted. If he saw it that way, then that's the way it was. And we had to do the changing.

The psychologist was able to help me get Mark out of the accelerated class. The principal didn't want to do it. She said, "Mrs. Lowry, you'll never get him back into the accelerated class if you take him out."

I said, "Good, I don't ever want him back in it."

My pediatrician told me that many children in accelerated classes were on tranquilizers.

Our school district was fourteenth in the nation at that time and proud of it.

David Elkind is a noted child psychologist at Tufts University in Massachusetts. He has written a book called *"The Hurried Child."* It talks about how we have put our children into a pressure cooker by making them learn things at an earlier and earlier age. The Japanese have done this to their children also and have the highest suicide rate among young people of any nation. Dr. Elkind has written another book on adolescence called, *"All Grown Up and No Place To Go."* You should make both of those books part of your library. When I read *"The Hurried Child"*, I thought David Elkind was a fundamental Baptist Preacher. He talks about the subliminal message in Rock Music. And what it is doing to our youth. But he is Jewish.

When Mark was put in the "average" class, I requested a "Mother-teacher." I wanted someone who could tell me what was normal and what wasn't.

Have you ever felt that way? If you have a child with any abnormal behavior, whether it is hyperactivity, learning disability or whatever, you have wanted to know that answer. What is normal?

I felt that a Mother-teacher could tell me that. I was right. Mrs. Ramona Hollan was the only third grade teacher who was also a Mother and she was teaching the "average" class.

Mrs. Hollan is a lovely Mother-type woman. She took Mark into her class and began to work with him. I fully credit her as being one of the turning points in his life. She was and still is a godly woman and really cared for her students. It showed in her actions with them and their actions with her. She had two children of her own. She has retired from teaching school and we still stay in touch.

She had a student teacher with her that semester. When Mark would become very antsy, Mrs. Hollan would take him to the schoolyard and walk around with him. She is a wonderful godly woman. She said they spent the whole semester discussing the Bible on those walks.

I became pregnant with my daughter in November 1966. The funny thing about that was that Mark had said to me that some people on our street were having babies and that if I would get a baby for our family, he would be good. Well, I did, and he lied, ha! He still had the same hyperactivity as before.

Mrs. Hollan kept telling me that Mark needed to be in the accelerated class. She said that when she gave an assignment he would hand it in and she would give it back to him and tell him that it was messy. He would hand it in again before the rest of the class handed it in the first time.

Mark saw a love in Mrs. Hollan that was rare in teachers. He knew that she cared about him and because of that he began to change.

She also wrote a musical that year for her class and Mark was the "star." I played the piano and they performed it for all of the other students in the school. During this time Mark was calming down a bit.

I saw something else happening for Mark. His creativity was beginning to bloom. He would write stories. Of course, he was always in them. But they actually made sense. His writing ability was in the budding stage.

This is the hyperactive boy who thirty years later wrote the song, "Mary Did You Know?"

I was always a room-mother for both of the boy's classes while they were in elementary school. I loved it. I would make things for the whole class. One Christmas I made ceramic snowman mugs for every child in the class and put their name on the snowman's hat. Another Christmas I made tree ornaments of Snoopy sleeping on his doghouse with his Christmas stocking hanging on the house. I made Easter baskets for every child. I loved it. I worked at the library and decorated the bulletin boards. I did everything I could to help my children know that I was there and wanted to be part of their lives. I also felt that if I got to know the teachers, that would somehow make things a little easier for Mark.

Some of the other Mothers and I would dress in costume and go through the rooms and give out candy to the children at Halloween. The year that Mark had been moved from Miss Johnson's class to Mrs. Hollan's, we swept into Miss Johnson's class. Sure enough she had all of her little third grade students sitting with their hands folded, listening to her lecture. I swept around Miss Johnson and swung her around and around. The class went wild. They started screaming and shouting. They were having a blast and I was too. I was dressed in a witch's costume and she didn't know who I was. She never knew until now, if she is reading this book. I'll bet it took her at least thirty minutes to get the class calmed down again after we left. Well, knowing her, it probably only took five minutes.

In a letter from Mrs. Hollan a few years ago, she said that Mark had kept them all informed that year about "having babies" because "Mama was pregnant."

Today I understand a lot that was taking place in Mark's life that year. It was wonderful that we were able to get that psychologist who knew that Mark needed firm limits (yes, discipline, at times) and encouragement.

I tell the women in the conferences in which I speak that a lot of people ask me how I raised Mark. I tell them, "I did not raise Mark. His Daddy raised him. He raised him five feet off the floor, (Sometimes). Discipline does work." (For whom the LORD loveth he correcteth; even as a father the son in whom he delighteth. Proverbs 3:12) (Correct thy son, and he shall give thee rest; yea, he shall give delight unto thy soul. Proverbs 29:13).

We thank God for allowing Mark to be placed in Mrs. Hollan's class and for the fact that she is a godly woman. She recognized his love of "entertaining" and she provided a way for him to do it for the whole school. He had an unusual voice for a child that age and he also had a need for competency. Mrs. Hollan supplied a way for him to use his talents and begin to feel competent. Competency comes for a child when they feel that they can do something well. Mark had found his niche.

If you have a Hyperactive Child, look for the child's niche and work with the child to fulfill his or her competency in that niche. It may be sports, music, art or whatever. They need to feel that they can do something that is really special for them.

*8-year-old Mark singing at a
Country Western performance*

*Mark, 9, Mike, 11, and baby sister, Melissa,
5 days old*

The following is a story that Mark's third grade teacher wrote and delivered to her Vacation Bible School Class and to other gatherings, the summer after having Mark in her third grade class, in Hollibrook Elementary School, Houston, Texas, in 1966-67. She graciously gave me permission to reprint it in this book. (THANK YOU AGAIN!, Mrs. Hollan)

About: Mark Alan Lowry
By: Mrs. Ramona Hollan (1966-67)

This is a true story about a little nine-year-old American boy. In fact, this little boy is a Texan. Can you guess what city he lives in? Yes, right here in Houston, Texas. We'll call this little boy Mark. I know this is a true story, because it happened right in my class at school, in third grade.

Mark was having quite a few problems in his classroom at school. He just couldn't seem to get himself settled. His classmates hated him and didn't want to sit by him or anything. I first learned of Mark when my principal told me that he was being moved to my room after the first six weeks of school this past year. She said that since Mark had gotten off to such a bad start and was so very unhappy and the class seemed to be progressing so much faster than he was that it might be better that he be moved to my room. She said, too, that since the other teacher was single and that since I was married and had a little boy of my

28

own that I might be able to figure out Mark's problem and help him.

It was on a Monday morning when I met Mark as the teacher next door brought him in and introduced him. He was a cute, clean-cut, neat little boy and I thought to myself, "Oh, we're going to get along fine!" We have always been told and reminded each year over and over by our principal and superintendent that "There is good in each child and it is your job to search for the good and bring out the good and then the evil or bad will have a way of disappearing!"

Things went along fine for the first week or so. Then, gradually, as he began to get acquainted he began to do some of the things that he had done in the other room. He began to pick on the other children, call them ugly names, talk aloud, run around the room, and just hundreds of other things that were against our rules. He would not listen to directions and would not follow directions. He made comments on the work and said it was "easy." The reason he thought it was so "easy" was that he was not taking his time and doing it correctly. As we walked down the hall he would swing around the poles, go the other directions (down the first grade hall, or fifth grade hall) and would just go the direction he wanted to go. On the playground, if he didn't like the way the game was going, he would take the ball and run off to the far corner of the playground so he could have the ball to himself.

It didn't take long for me to see what the other teacher meant when she said, "He'll drive you crazy!" I spent a lot of my day searching for him, making him come into the room, making him go out at recess with the other children—praying for patience, that I'd know just exactly what to do with him and how to get "through to him" as we say in elementary school. I had punished him in several ways, I had talked with his parents—and was informed by his mother, "He does some of these same things in the neighborhood." It was then that I was beginning to get some clues to Mark's behavior. When other children in the neighborhood were bad their parents punished them by making them stay in their own yard or house and not letting them play with others until they could be good. I talked with Mark's Cub Scout leader about his conduct in Scouts and was told, "Oh, Mrs. Hollan, I know what you're going through with Mark. We can hardly have scouts because he is constantly disrupting, wanting to be 'THE ONLY ONE.' One day our son was bad and misbehaved something terrible. His punishment was that he could not go out of the yard for a week. He could have his friends over, but could not go anywhere. Mark came over to visit our son. Can you imagine the shock when Mark told my husband, 'You sure are mean parents by making your son stay in the yard. My mother loves me and never makes me do anything when I get bad grades or do something wrong.' My husband and I did not know what to say, but we believe children should obey their parents."

This is the way Mark treated grown-ups. He didn't mind telling them anything. He talked just as ugly and sassy to grown-ups as he did to children.

I worked and worked with Mark trying to get him to understand that we have to have some rules at school. Have you ever driven way out in the country where there are no paved streets? You do not see any traffic lights. Can you imagine how it would be if there were none in our cities today? Rules and laws have to be made for the protection and safety of all people. It would not have mattered if Mark had done all the loud talking, the running around the room and other things if he had been my only student. But I had twenty-four others. They were just as important as he was—but this was the one thing that he could not see!

After talking with Mark's parents about his behavior another time, they asked that I take him to the office for a spanking when he misbehaved again. They said they had asked the teacher next door to do this when he was in her class but she never had. I told them that if this was what they wanted, then I certainly would do that. Well, it didn't take long for him to misbehave again. I said, "Mark, come with me." He said, "Where are we going?" and I told him that we were going to the office. I don't know what he thought, but he marched along just like a little man. (His mother had told me earlier that he probably would not go, that I'd have to drag him down there and I knew I didn't want to do that.) Anyway, we went to the office, the principal talked with him as she had done many, many times before. However, this time she gave him a good hard spanking. This helped for about a week. Then, gradually, he started some of his old habits again. This is the thing that is so bad about habits—especially bad habits. Once we have them, it is very, very hard to get rid of them. We have to work constantly to get rid of them and to change our attitude.

I saw the parents at P.T.A. meeting about a month later and they asked how Mark was doing. I had to tell them that he was doing okay as far as his schoolwork was concerned. He was an above-average boy, in fact he was quite smart. He could get his work done in half the time required for most of the other students. His father was an attorney, his mother was very talented, could play the piano, make beautiful ceramics, was a Scout leader, etc., so Mark had traveled quite a bit, been around, and knew quite a bit. Then, I had to also tell the parents that Mark's conduct was still very poor. These were the words the father said to me, "Look Mrs. Hollan, we've got to get this problem straightened out. We can't let a little nine-year-old boy ruin our lives, his life and everyone's life. We're going to try the old-fashioned method of punishment. If he misbehaves again, take him to the office and wear him out. Do this each time he misbehaves. When you have done that, get on the phone and call me and I can assure you that he'll get the same punishment at home. We have tried to get it through his head that he must behave at school. Since we can't get it through his head then maybe we can get it through the seat of his pants!" He said, "Will you do it?" I told him that I would if that was the way they wanted it handled. I asked that they please be consistent with their punishment and treatment of him at home, because I was beginning to think that this was part of his problem. He just didn't know what NO meant. I would tell him NO in answer to a question and his reply was, "If I beg you, can I?" Have you ever asked Mother if you could do something and she in turn said, "Go ask your Daddy." Then, when you went to ask your Daddy, he'd say—"Go ask your Mother." I used to spend many an hour going from my mother to my Daddy until I learned that if neither of them would say NO that they probably didn't care one way or another or neither was up to making a decision, so I took the answer to be YES. I told Mom, after having been to Daddy and being sent to Mom, "I guess I can go or I guess I can do it because Daddy said to ask you and you said to ask Daddy, and since neither of you can give me an answer YES or NO, I'll just ask ME and I would always say YES. I hope parents will teach children the meaning of NO. Mean no when you say no and stick by it. If you don't intend to mean no, just say maybe.

I continued to have a little trouble working with Mark because I had a student teacher from the University of Houston. He tried some of these same things with her that he tried with me and all the talking and pleading that she did with him did no good. I really did not feel that I should take him and punish him when she was doing the teaching, but I knew we had to get this problem straightened out. I had more time to study him and his records since she was doing much of the teaching and I was just observing. I consulted his permanent record and found that his kindergarten teacher had commented, "A problem child—sassy, bull-headed. Received a spanking." Reading further, his first grade teacher had commented—"Is a show-off, can't sit still. Received a spanking." Reading further, his second grade teacher had commented, "Always wants to be the center of attention. Does great when he gets his own way."

Well, I kept my promise to Mark's Dad. The next time he disturbed and disobeyed when I was teaching I gave him a good little warning and told him, "We'd take a trip", if things continued to get worse. And they did get worse! One day he dusted another boy's face with the chalk eraser. He also colored his own face with black crayon to look like a clown. I told him to go wash it off and not do it again. He deliberately did it again while I was not looking. So, we took our little trip just as I had promised and he got another good hard spanking. I called his Dad and he got the same treatment at home. He was the best little boy in my class for a week or so and then BAD HABITS APPEARED AGAIN. Gradually some of what we were trying to get through was getting through because he would look to see if I was around before he would do some of the things or he would look at me to see the expression on my face. I could shake my head no, and many times he would not do these bad things. The meaning of NO was beginning to get through, at least at school. He was getting rid of some of his old bad habits. He was not putting snakes and bugs on little girls any longer. I had talked him into making a wire cage to bring to the room so that we could watch the snakes and bugs, which he caught at recess. We could then study them and learn something from them. This did prove to be a learning experience. I'll never forget the day he caught a snake. It was about eighteen inches long. It was larger than many of the grass snakes, which we had seen, but I was not sure as to the kind, however, I knew it was not poisonous. I asked him to put it in his cage and to leave it alone. You know, most girls are afraid of snakes and most boys like to torment them, so I knew that if he took it out there would be trouble. Well, bad habit crept in again. While the class was in the auditorium singing, Mark hung around the room. He did just what I told him not to do. He got the snake out of its cage and was looking at it and playing with it. While he was doing this about six inches of the snake's tail broke off right in Mark's hand! I heard a commotion in the hall and there stood Mark. He had run down the hall with the snake in one hand and the snake's tail in another hand. There was the most shocked look on his face that I have ever seen. Needless to say, music class was over and he threw the tail of the snake across the playground, just as far as he could throw it. He said, "Oh, look at all that blood—do you think I have hurt the snake, do you think the snake will die—I don't want the snake to die, I want to have it for my pet." After I finally calmed him down, we had a science lesson on snakes and we searched until we finally found the kind of snake—it was a GLASS SNAKE. A characteristic of this snake is that when it is caught it can break a part of its tail off and slither away from its enemy. I showed the class the pictures and read them the story and finally convinced Mark that he had not killed his snake. The tail would grow back, but it would take time. Well, even though he disobeyed this time, I did not punish him because I felt that he had learned his lesson because he had almost lost something he wanted very much.

He got several other spankings this year; one because he threw milk all over a little girl in the cafeteria, and another for telling lies and using very ugly language.

When Mark first came to our room he wouldn't sing or participate with the class. It was not until he had been in our room for about two months that he would even join in with the games or anything. Gradually he began to sing, then the children heard his voice ring out with the others. One could definitely tell that the child had an outstanding voice. The children asked him to sing by himself. He first said no, so I asked him and he still said no. I then said, "Well, we're not going to beg you. The children want you to sing, and I want you to sing, but if you don't want to sing that's okay with us." A few days later he said to me and the class, "Well, if you really want me to sing, I will." And he did—a beautiful song.

I knew that Mark was very talented. He had a beautiful voice. His mother had worked with him and he could really sing! We put on a program, "All about

March" for the other four third-grade classes and he sang two or three songs. The children just loved to hear him sing. They begged to have music every day, just so they could hear Mark sing. I liked it too, because when Mark was singing he seemed to have a different personality—to be a very, different child. Some time later just after music, we went outside to play. Someone said, "Let Mark be leader." I said, "Well, I'm not sure Mark can lead, he hasn't paid attention to the exercises very carefully." Often he would just wander around during play period or even dance around or turn flips, etc. when we were learning new games or exercises. But I said, "Okay, if he wants to try." He said, "Sure, I can do it." And he did! He did a beautiful job. I had tried before to get him to do things, but he never would.

This was his good—this was it! This was really his best—I had at last found the BEST in him and in order to get rid of the BAD, we had to let more of the BEST show. We had music in our classroom more than the allotted time, but I was working on a problem—a problem which had existed for a long time—since kindergarten or before! We didn't neglect our other studies, but we had music almost every day for a little while and some of Mark's songs became the favorites of the class.

Mark had friends. They wanted to sing with him, so I'd let two or three boys sing specials. After all, one can't neglect a whole classroom of children just because of one.

Others found out about Mark's talents and soon he was asked to sing some specials for the P.T.A. meeting in April. There were a lot of people there and he was to sing, then a minister from one of our churches was to speak to the people. He marched to the stage like a little gentleman, all dressed up in a navy blue sport coat, grey pants, a red design on his coat, and a red handkerchief in his pocket. He was neat, clean, every hair was in place. In fact, he was about the best looking little boy you have ever seen any place. He sang two or three popular songs and the parents and teachers really liked it. What clapping there was as he finished and started to go down the hall to the children's room to be with the baby sitter. Then someone said, "Bring him back; let him sing two more." That's what they did and his next song was, "He's Got the Whole World in His Hands." You could hear a pin drop in that auditorium. He had a beautiful voice—his song had a beautiful message! The teacher next to me whispered, "Isn't he precious, I've never seen such a lovely child! Whose room is he in?" I told her that he was in my room, and about that time he started singing his last song, which went something like this:

You laid your hand, mighty Lord, on the range
Laid your wonderful hand on the prairie
Lord, you poured forth the fountains,
Raised up the mountains
Oh! Lord keep your mighty hand on me.
You touched your clouds, made them rain
From the rain made the sea, from the sea formed the
    clouds

To give us life abundantly:
You have the earth and the sky in your command,
   Lord
Oh! Please keep your precious hand on me!

There were tears in the eyes of some of the people as he finished singing. Later people told me how his singing had touched them. Here then was a child who had a two-fold personality. One time, he was very, very bad, hurting others very much. At another time, when he was singing and had the right attitude, he was helping others very much. The Lord began to show me right there just how I was going to get through to this child. As he sang this song, it became a prayer for me. I asked the Lord right there in that P.T.A. meeting to keep his hand on that child. I asked the Lord to help him to be the kind of person every day that he was that night when he was singing.

Earlier in the year Mark's Mother had said to me, "You're a Christian, aren't you, Mrs. Hollan?" How did she know? My principal didn't tell her, I know. I didn't tell her. But you can tell a person is a real Christian, can't you? I told his Mother that, "Yes, I am a Christian." She said, "I could tell", and she asked me where I went to church. One day while we were having math, right out of the clear blue sky Mark said, "Mrs. Hollan, (he raised his hand, he'd learned that!) my Mother says that you're a Christian. How can she tell?" Well, since it was in the middle of math lesson, I told him that I would talk with him later and I did after school. There are two things that we're not supposed to talk about at school—that is about our religion and politics you know, like who you voted for, for governor or president. Well, I can get by without telling about that so much, especially with third graders, but I can't get by very well without talking about God. When you really feel something in your heart you want to live it each day and talk about it. I could see then, after the song and after I found that Mark's parents were Christians that this was going to be my way "through to this child."

Since I had a student teacher and could leave the room now for long stretches of time, I had a chance to get to talk with Mark more and more. He had not gotten rid of all his Bad Habits. When you have done things for four or five years, it takes time to get rid of them. He continued to do things that were bad. When this happened one day, I took him outside and we went for a walk. An elementary school is a very busy place and it's always hard to find a place where there is complete quietness. This I wanted so Mark wouldn't miss anything that I had to say to him. We walked and looked for empty rooms, but they were all filled. We had just completed lunch, but there was another group in the cafeteria so we couldn't talk there.

The student teacher was teaching for the next two hours so I knew I had plenty of time to talk and I was determined to get to the bottom of his problem. We finally wandered to the playground and sat down under a big shady tree, just Mark and God and me, plus the wonderful things all around that God had made.

My first question was, "Mark, why do you act like you do?" He looked at me sort of funny as if he wasn't going to answer and then said, "I don't know what you're talking about." I said, "Oh, don't give me that! You know exactly what I'm talking about." You have been making bad, bad grades in conduct ever since you started to school. Why don't you behave? Why don't you be nice like other boys and girls? Why can't you treat others the way they treat you? Why must you take away their valuable rights, especially the right to learn? Why do you steal?"

Mark's eyes lit up—I was getting through. He said, "I don't steal!" He was angry. I had to make him angry to get him to talking to get it through to him just what I meant. He said, "When did I ever steal anything, just tell me when it was and what it was! Mrs. Hollan, you know we go to church because my Mother told you. We go to church twice on Sunday and on Wednesday nights, too. I sing in the Junior choir. You know I'd never steal anything!"

I just sat there, letting him think over what I'd said. Then I said, "What about time? Every time you've talked and disturbed others you've stolen their time, their right to learn. When you say ugly words you steal someone's clean thoughts by filling their mind with dirty thoughts. When you pinch or hit someone you're taking away the right to keep a nice, clean healthy body—because you can make an ugly bruise or a broken part of the body. When you take the ball and run to the other side of the playground, you're stealing someone else's right to play with his classmates and have a good time. When you misbehave all the time and the teacher has to spend more time with you than with anyone else, you're stealing the teacher's time that each child in the classroom is entitled to." I told him, "Right now, you're stealing my time." This also made him mad. "You don't have to be here with me, you don't have to be wasting your time like this!"

I told him that I knew that I didn't have to spend my time doing this, but that I was because I wanted to do it. He asked me why I wanted to do it and I told him I was doing it because I loved him, and I wanted to see him grow up to be a fine young man. I told him if he continued in the same way he was going that he would end up in jail, or some place bad. The way he sassed his parents and talked back to and made fun of adults, he would continue doing the same as he got older and pretty soon do it to policemen and other officers and end up in jail.

He started crying, the first tears I'd seen all year except for the snake. Sure, he had gotten four or five spankings this year. He was smart enough to tell me later that "They only hurt for a while and then the hurt wears off." With tears in his eyes, he started telling me his story.

When I was just a little boy, I realized that my brother (now age 11) could do many things that I could not do. I wanted to be just like him. He could climb trees, he could swim very fast, he could throw a ball and do all the things that boys like to do. I was always too little, too short, too slow! I guess to make up for it, I just go around pushing, shoving, and especially talking loud and ugly. This is the one thing that I can do and do well. This is the main thing that gets me in trouble. My brother has played on the Little League Baseball team. I never get to play on any team. I couldn't even throw a ball, hit a ball, or jump a rope until I got in your room and you worked and worked with me and made me get out there and play. My other teachers just let me do what I wanted to do because I was "too much trouble" to bother with. You made me get out there and play. You worked and worked with me until I could jump a rope, then continued to work until I could hit that ball. I felt so proud.

The kids in the neighborhood will let me play with them now because I'm not afraid of the ball and can hit it and run like the rest of them. I'm also learning to take my turn. I guess I did all those ugly things because I had a yearning to be like my brother and couldn't.

I told him the story of how I too, as a youngster, had wanted to be like my sister, who is three years older. I wanted to be like her more than anything else in the world. She always got to do things that I never got to do because she was older. Now, many years later, the tables have turned. Many times my sister has remarked, "I wish I could be like you. You finished high school, I dropped out and got married at the age of sixteen. You went to college and got an education.

43

Now you have a nice family and a job so that you can be home with your family in the summer." You never know about things like..."Wanting to be like someone."

I then reminded Mark that God did not intend us to all be alike. Sure, I told him, our aim is to be like Christ. Prov. 20:11. He added, "No one is perfect." I told him that I knew this, that it was always hard to keep from making mistakes and doing things that were not good, but you could constantly ask God to help you if you were a Christian. It was then that I asked him the question "Mark, are you a Christian?" "Living in the church house does not make you a Christian, just as a bird living in a hornets' nest does not make him a hornet. Christ has to be living in your life. If you, with the help of Christ, do not change your bad habits, then it must be time to ask yourself, "Am I really a Christian?"

We talked a long time about many things the Lord had done and could do. I reminded him that his brother was talented in sports and that he was talented in other ways. He had a beautiful voice. I told him how proud of him I was when he sang those songs at P.T.A. But I also told him what the minister had said, too. He said, "I think it's grand that a youngster like Mark has such a talent and the teachers and parents want him to use his talents." He said he hoped Mark used his talent in the church (and he does by singing specials and sings in the choir) but he said, "You know, Mark may have a lovely voice and be a great musician, but he may be bad in another subject, such as math." I told Mark how I felt, how I wanted to stand up and wave my hands and say, "Folks, let me tell you about Mark. It's not his math that he is bad in—he is just bad, bad, bad. He needs to have Christ in his life so that he can control his life all day, every day, not just in church or when he's singing for God or about God."

Mark kept telling me, "But I want to be big like my brother because everyone likes him. He's so nice and can do so many things." Then I made the remark, "Well, you can't, because you're just a baby!" This made him mad, too. You see, I had worked with this child long enough to know that only when he got mad would he really listen to me and talk to me. At other times he would just close up and not say a word.

"I'm not a baby, I'm nine years old." "Oh," I said, "you're not a baby—just how big are you? Are you big enough and strong enough to be the Mark that God wants you to be and not try anymore to be like your brother? God made you and he made you different. If God had intended you to be like your brother, don't you think he'd have sent your mother and daddy twins, instead of waiting two years later to send you along?" (My message was getting through!) "God wants you to be YOU!" "He has made you different."

"Yes," he interrupted, "the pastor often says that the Bible says that 'Wherefore come ye out from among them, and be ye separate, saith the Lord.' But," he said, "I thought that meant that we were not to do the things that sinners and people of the world do." I told him, "Yes, God intends us to be a separate people, a different people. Maybe that's the reason your mother knew that I was a Christian. She could tell that I was different from the other people, yet at the same time, as we are all striving to be Christians and Christlike we have to each do it in our own way. We can't all sing specials, we can't all play the piano, but we can all do our best and be our best for Jesus no matter where we go." I reminded Mark that his playmates could not tell that he was a Christian. He was the meanest little boy in the class, even in the whole school. Was that being Christlike? Pushing, shoving, stealing, using ugly language, talking back to his Mother and Father, his teachers, etc—to be a Christian one must strive to be like Christ. He must honour his Father and Mother (and those that teach him and take the place of Mother when she's not there) and he must love his neighbors as well as his enemies.

Mark made a promise right then and there to me, and I asked him to make it to God also that he would start being the kind of Christian that God would want him to be—all the time! I told him that if he thought he was big and strong he'd have to prove it, because you have to be big and strong to get rid of the habits which you have had for a long time. I told him he'd have to start doing things for others—thinking of others, not just himself. Jesus went about doing good, helping the sick and the lame and raising them up. Jesus did not think of himself. He thought of others. He even gave

His life for others—that we might live and have life more abundantly—like you, Mark, sang in your song.

Mark asked me if I was going to call his Father about our "conference under the tree" because he'd been so bad. I told him, "No, I'll not call him. This promise is just between you, God, and me. If anyone does the telling, it will be you." But, I reminded him that I expected to see just How BIG he really was the rest of the school year. I told him that since his Mother had been sick he could start by helping at home, doing things without being asked. He reminded me that often, even though his job was to get in the trashcans, his Father would have to do it because he "forgot to do his job". That was the only job he had at home, but I reminded him also that there were many things a nine year old could do at home to help out. I reminded him, also, that his language must show that he is a Christian. The way he treated others should show that he loved them and that he has Christ in his life. The Bible tells us "Thou shalt not steal." This means anything and time is certainly a thing!

His last words to me that day were, "Mrs. Hollan, I'm bigger than you think I am. I'm bigger than my brother in a few ways. I'll prove to you for the rest of the year just how big I am."

Things improved greatly. His life is changing, but it's taking time, and, most important, it's taking GOD in his life to make the change. Only God can change our life completely.

Later during the school year I saw Mark's Mother and she said, "Mrs. Hollan, what in the world did you tell Mark?" I avoided her question (because I had promised him I would not tell) and I said, "Why?" Her remark was, "Well, the other day as we were riding to town he had several of his little friends in the back seat. I heard him tell them that his life was changed, that he was a different person." She said that she had noticed a difference in Mark in the neighborhood and in his manner at home. Again she asked me, "Mrs. Hollan, what did you say to Mark?" I told her that we'd just had a little talk and that if she really wanted to know that she'd have to ask Mark. I had made a promise to him and I expected to keep it." I don't know if Mark ever told his Mother or not; that's not real important. The important thing is that Mark's life has changed—not because of me, not because he's in church, but because God is IN Mark!

It's important that you stay in church, yes! It's more important that God stays in you! If God stays in your life then your life will shine and you'll be the kind of Christian God wants you to be—when, where—7/ days a week, 24 hours a day, EVERYWHERE YOU GO!

Mark's 3rd grade class, Hollibrook Elementary,
Spring Branch School District, Houston, Texas
Mrs. Ramona Hollan, teacher, in center
Student teacher on far left
1967

When Ramona Hollan's children heard Mark's video in which he stated that Mrs. Hollan, his third grade teacher, was ten years older than God, they insisted that she go and get "glamour" shots made and send them to Mark.

With the pictures she enclosed a note to Mark: *This was the way I looked when I taught you in 3rd grade at Hollibrook Elementary in 1966-67. The other picure was taken in 1997! How does your third grade picture compare with your "now" picture?*

Mark in 3rd grade, 1966-67   *Mark in 1997*

Why can't I be Me?
Written by Mark Lowry
in the 3rd Grade in 1966-67

My life is not my own
I really don't know why
If I could be somebody else
My life might be my own.
Why couldn't I be something else
Like a Lion or an Eagle If I was
one of them my life might be
My own
I really wouldn't want to be
a Lion or an Eagle but
there is something bothering me
Why can't I be Me

Thank You Letter To Mrs. Hollan

Dear Mrs. Hollan:

It was very good to hear from you. We all enjoyed the story about Mark. Mark said, "I'll bet she didn't write anything about the good boys." The story brought back many memories. Mark was quite a problem. I believe he told you what was really bothering him that day. It took a psychologist to get the message over to his Dad, but he finally got it and that helped Mark a lot. As you said would happen the tide did turn and when Mark was singing and traveling all over the country we had a little bit of the same problem with Mike. He was able to handle it better because of his age.

We got a big laugh out of Mark telling the neighbor in the story that his Mother loved him and would never punish him for making bad grades or getting in trouble. He said, "I was a liar, too." That was the year I was pregnant with Melissa and he probably did get by with more then because I was sick the whole nine months.

We've always considered the year in your class as one of the turning points in Mark's life. Probably the first.

The second one was when he was taken out of school in the eighth grade to sing in Gospel Music Concerts around the country. He was out of school for a year and a half taking correspondence. Then in the last part of the ninth grade, January 1972, we discovered that Melissa had sugar diabetes. We had a three-week tour scheduled for Florida the last week of January and first of February. One morning as I was changing Melissa's bed, my hand touched a spot where she had wet. It had dried and was stiff as if I'd sprayed it with starch. We were to leave for Florida the next week. The Lord impressed me to take a urine sample in for testing, which I did. On Wednesday she was put in the hospital and by Saturday morning they had the diagnosis: Sugar diabetes. Six doctors lined up in her room wanted to know how I had found it. I told them that God had certainly impressed me about this. They just kind of looked at me. But, I know God was in it because she never even got sick. They said most parents bring the children to the hospital in a coma and that she was passing acetones and would have been in a coma within the next three weeks. We would have been in the middle of Florida. God had certainly spared us a tragedy. She is almost eight now and looks healthy as a horse. But we give her an insulin shot every morning. Pray with me that God will heal her. Anyway, with this news we knew that until I knew how to take care of her, we would need to stay close to home. Mark went back to school at North Houston Christian School. He loved it. I believe his being out of school for a year & a half was the second turning point in his life because he was so glad to be back in school. His grades came up and even his conduct was so much better we could hardly believe it. He still sang a lot in Florida during the summer and in churches here in Texas on weekends.

In June of 1972, the greatest turning point of all came at a Church Camp in Nacagdoches, Texas. Mark was leading the singing that week. On Tuesday night Mike got saved. We had all known that he had doubted his salvation. And we were so thrilled for him to get it all settled. There were two services that night and between the services as Mark was talking to a deaf girl, Debbie, he told her something that he had never admitted to anyone else. He didn't know for sure if he had ever let Jesus come into his life. He got on his knees and asked the Lord to save him and He did. Boy, the change that came over him was a miracle. The next week we were scheduled for a tour in West Texas. Mark sang an hour concert and told what God had done for him and two teenage girls were saved. He gives the invitation himself and it's marvelous the way God is using him. During the last two years, I can't tell you how many hearts and lives have been touched by God through Mark. He still has a very dogmatic attitude, but God is using that for His glory. Mark is very firm in his beliefs. And he truly loves the Lord.

As I look back over his life, I can see how God had His hand on Mark. And He still does. He will be going to Lynchburg Baptist College in Lynchburg, Virginia this fall. If you watch Channel 26 on Sunday at 1:30 you may see him sometime. If I know when he's on, I'll call you. Mark will be singing in churches up there on the weekends. They will book him out of the College and he can pay his own way through school that way. Mike attended the same college last year and grew so much spiritually. Mike plays about five different string instruments, including the 5-string banjo and steel guitar. He has a group at college called "True Vine" and they travel into area churches singing for the Lord. So the Lord has really worked things out for us. Our two boys, one almost twenty and the other just turned seventeen have never given us one bit of trouble like the other teens in our neighborhood. Neither one has ever even tried drugs or been in trouble with the police. Their friends have always been the kids in our church and other than being determined to have their own way at times, they have been sons that anyone would be proud of.

Thank you so much for that seven months that you spent with Mark and the help you gave him. I only wish we had more teachers like you who really care what happens to a child after they leave their room. This is really what being a Christian teacher means.

Mike and Mark both graduated from our own Church school, Greenwood Village Christian School. Melissa is going there now and I teach piano and choir there. The teachers there do care about their students.

Thank you again for your influence in Mark's life. I just wanted you to know that the many prayers offered for him have been answered. Praise God! There were many times when we felt all we *could* do was pray. But God is faithful. I always claimed the promise, "Train up a child in the way he should go and when he is old, he'll not depart from it." So many misinterpret that to mean that if they do stray, they'll come back. But that's not what it says. It says they'll *not depart* from it. I'm so grateful to God for His promises. If we keep our part—He always keeps His.

We love you,

Beverly & Charles Lowry
and family

Chapter Three

Finding The Mark
(Knowledge, Wisdom and Hope)

I knew that God was working in his life as a nine-year-old boy.

I didn't know anything about psychology. I didn't know that Erik Erikson says that from six to puberty that a child will have a crisis in their life and either develops industry or inferiority. I didn't know that in Phil Captain's theory of Christian psychology (The Alpha Omega Process) the child has the need to learn obedience from age two to six. Dr. Captain says that rebellion is normal at that age and abnormal in the teen-age years. The time to deal with rebellion is from the age of two to six. They have the need to develop competence from the age of six to twelve. Erik Erikson also says that. Failure to develop competence in the middle childhood years will lead to feeling inferior. I didn't know that when we were struggling with the problem. But God did. He wrote the psychology book. If anything is true in psychology it's because God set the stages of development because He is the creator of the universe.

And I was praying constantly for my little boys, Mike and Mark. I wanted them to be liked. I wanted them to have friends. Mike made friends pretty easily. I knew that Mark was a wonderful person with a big heart. He just didn't know how to deal with all of the things going on inside of him.

I made a lot of mistakes. I wish I had looked through his eyes sometimes and said, "Well, how does he see this situation?"

I wish I had not cared so much what other people thought. I felt that people around me were judging me as a Mother all the time. Later in my college years, (I started to college at the age of forty-six), I would learn that all Moms feel this way. We all have a psychological need to be good Moms. But I want to tell young Mothers today, "Don't worry about other people. The only One you need to please in raising your children is God. He gave them to you for a purpose. Please Him and Him alone." I don't even know most of those people today. I live 1,300 miles from all of them. Don't be embarrassed by your children. Their conduct doesn't make you a good or bad Mother or Father. They have a sin nature and you have a sin nature. That means you will not always do everything perfect or be a perfect parent. They are not extensions of your hands. God has really used this hyperactive boy to help other hyperactive boys and girls. God has allowed Mark to do something with his life. He is serving God.

Yes, I was a screamer. Maybe not exactly like Mark plays it up. Sometimes I was just trying to be louder than the boys were. But James Dobson says that screaming doesn't make you a bad parent. I really did feel that I had failed and said so to my children. Again I was so hung up on what other people thought.

I did some things right. I stood up for him when I thought he was right. Oh, I never criticized a teacher or other adult to him. I wanted him to respect authority when he was a teenager or adult. But I defended him to them when I felt that they were wrong. I would get an appointment and go behind closed doors and talk to them. I think that permanent records being passed from one teacher to another is wrong. A teacher should not look at those records until near the end of the semester. She should make up her own mind. A child can change during the summer. He could have gotten saved at Church camp. But we force them right back into the same mold. It's hard to change when you're an adult much less when you're a child. We tend to act the way we are expected to act. So let's give children the opportunity to change.

Don't be afraid to defend your child. They were loaned to you by God and you need to be their advocate. They can't stand up to a teacher, but you can. And I don't mean that you go in and fuss at a teacher. The teacher has a hard job. And we do have to realize that most of the time the teacher is right.

I empathize with teachers in Elementary and Jr. High School today. Sometimes the parents think their child can do no wrong. I saw a cartoon one day where the little boy came home from school and said, "Mama, I made an F in math because I said 2 plus 2 is five." The Mama said, "Don't worry, we'll get an attorney." That is sad. When I went to talk to a teacher, I prayed first and then went in a quiet manner and asked for her help. In talking I would often times find that the teacher was right. If the teacher was wrong, I would say so gently.

I prayed. I asked God for wisdom all the time. I claimed Prov. 22:6 "Train up a child in the way he should go; and when he is old, he will not depart from it."

I used to say that God gave me that promise, and I believe He did, and that if my children didn't stay straight it was because I had failed to train them and not because God had not kept His promise. I took that verse very seriously.

We had our children in church every time the doors opened. We lived our faith seven days a week.

We loved Mark and he knew it.

Charles and I stood united in our discipline. (Charles backed me when he came home from work). We structured Mark's life. I could go on and on about those struggles but I want to give you some hope. Hope comes as we trust and have faith in God. We all want to be able to see the future. But if we could see the future we wouldn't need any faith. The Bible says that without faith it's impossible to please God. So we have to do everything we can and trust God for the outcome.

I believe that you are trying to be good parents and you are concerned about your children or you wouldn't be reading this book. Quite frankly I would have loved to have heard an older woman tell me that Mark would turn out all right when he was in the third grade. Titus 2:3-4 says that the aged women should teach the young women to love their husbands and to love their children. I used to wonder as a young Mother how anyone could teach me to love my husband and children more than I did. But today we live such a fast-paced life that sometimes you will have to work at having time to show your children that you love them. We know that we love them but they can't read minds. We have to tell them and more than that we have to show them.

Let me say here that there are three kinds of attention:

1. Positive attention: Rewards, hugs, kisses, money. Things like that.

2. Negative attention: Spanking, fussing at them.

3. No attention: Ignoring them.

They will choose negative attention over no attention. They had rather be spanked than ignored. So if you have a child that seems to be out of control, make sure that you are giving them some positive attention. Sometimes when a child does what we want them to do, we ignore it. We don't praise them for making their bed; they are supposed to make their bed. Don't remake their bed. If you do, that is making a statement. They didn't do it good enough.

We all need encouragement; they are no different.

Put the word **"Encourage"** on your refrigerator door. Dr. Ken West, my professor at Lynchburg College, (the year I took his course) said he had never counseled an out of control child who wasn't a discouraged child.

We all need to be encouraged. Your children do too. For every time that you have to use negative attention, spanking or fussing, use positive attention three times. They are your children; surely you can find something good to say to them. They should not have to earn our love. We love them because they are our children. Isn't that the way God loves us? Give positive attention as much as possible. Try to give less negative attention. Sometimes try other ways to discipline, such as natural and logical consequences and some time-outs in their room. They are not miniature adults. We have to teach them. And a lot of what we teach them will be taught in the way we model for them. They will handle stress in much the same way they see us handle stress. They will be polite and considerate and have social graces if we model those things in our own lives. Children are like wet cement, everything they see leaves an imprint on them. I once saw a sign in Idaho that said, "Good character is like good soup, it's made at home."

We can teach social graces, such as shoveling snow for an older neighbor, helping others in need and showing love to others.

Telling a child that I am going to tell you one time is ridiculous. They are limited in how they think by their cognitive development. You will tell them many times before they learn.

You may teach them to respond to you the first time you speak, but I found in teaching piano that real teaching takes saying the same thing over and over many times.

Our children are no different.

I know that you are like I was and you want to be a perfect parent. Forgive yourself for not being one. There are none. We all have sin natures and because of that sometimes we are going to lose our cool. We may even raise our voice at them.

But if we are really trying to be good parents and trying to train them in the way God wants us to, then we will be diligent in our training as it says in Deut.6: 5 "And thou shalt love the Lord thy God with all thine heart and with all thy soul and with all thy might. v. 6 And these words, which I command thee this day, shall be in thine heart: v.7 And thou shalt teach them diligently unto thy children, and shalt talk of them when thou sittest in thine house and when thou walkest by the way and when thou liest down, and when thou riseth up." ALL THE TIME.

Parenting isn't easy. It is one of the hardest jobs in the world.

So what am I saying? Relax. You are not going to be a perfect parent. But you will be a good one. Someday you will want that little child hanging on to your skirt or pants leg for a friend.

They will be your best friends.

They will turn out all right if you are a good parent and teach them by your life and actions to love God with all their heart.

My little hyperactive child is a great encourager to people. He feels that his ministry is to people as he travels the country talking about his own struggles and ours as his parents in raising him.

And his videos have helped many children to know that they can serve God. They have helped some teachers to see that they could be teaching someone who will serve God later in their life. And teachers are not forgotten. I still remember my first grade teacher, Miss Milner.

I often say, "Be careful how you treat those children or you may end up on a video some day."

I have had many people ask me: "How do you feel when he is up there making jokes about you?" God and His wonderful leadership in Mark's life awe me. And I thank God everyday for leading us as his parents and actually allowing us to have him as our child for such a short time. Childhood is over too quickly.

I love what I am doing today. I love teaching at Liberty University and I love speaking in Ladies Conferences around the country, but I would live those days as a young Mother over in a minute if I had the chance. They were the best. I am sorry that many Mothers are missing those years for a career. I am so happy that I was encouraged by my husband to be a stay-at-home Mom.

A few years ago Mark wrote this in his newsletter.

"How I Know I'm Not Perfect:

Do all kids think their parents are perfect? I did. When I was a small child my parents could do no wrong. I thought my dad was the tallest and my Mother was always right. But, then I hit puberty. That changed everything. My dad was an inch shorter than me, and my Mother had very little practical sense, or so I thought. It was quite a revelation to find out your parents aren't perfect.

Then I found out I'm not perfect. I'm reminded everyday how imperfect I am. My imperfect brain thinks imperfect thoughts almost constantly.

The other day I was flying to Grand Rapids, Michigan and I was sitting next to this little old lady. I knew she was old 'cause her teeth were brand new. She was propped up against the window sound asleep. I knew she was in a deep sleep because her mouth was hanging open and she was drooling on herself. I had this awful urge to slap the side of her chair and scream in her ear, "We're crashing!!! Don't you care?" More proof that I'm not perfect.

When I heard about the first imperfect person, Eve, I was really mad at her. I thought if she hadn't eaten that fruit in the Garden of Eden we'd all be perfect and still living there. I used to think when I get to Heaven I'm gonna slap her! But you know, if Eve had not eaten that fruit and all the humans who had ever lived had not eaten it, I probably would have been the first to take a bite and mess up the whole thing. I'm not perfect.

Only one Person has made it all the way through His life without "taking the bite." His name is Jesus. He never sassed His mom. He never took anything that didn't belong to Him. He grew as a teenager "in favor with God and man," the Bible says.

And His perfection ticked people off. So, finally they nailed Him to a cross. His death paid for our sins. But, we still sin. We're still not perfect. Wouldn't it be nice if when you received Jesus into your life all of a sudden you were perfect! Now, there are those who think they're perfect. They think they've reached some high level of sanctification and no longer sin. But what is sin? Sin is any time you don't measure up to God's standards. It isn't just running off with the deacon's wife. It isn't just cheating on your income taxes. It isn't just murdering the deacon so you can legally run off with his wife. Sin is anytime you miss the mark. I think we have this misconception of what sin is. Our best compared to His worst is still filthy rags. We just don't measure up. So, God sent Jesus to measure up for us. And, He who knew no sin became sin for us. Isn't that something? He didn't just somehow mysteriously pay for our sins. He became our sin. He became everything we didn't measure up to, so that we could, through Him, measure up.

No, I'm not perfect. If I were I'd tell you. But God promised that the good work He has begun in us He will complete!

One day He'll finish the job and we'll be perfect! Phil 1:6 "being confident of this, that he who began a good work in you will carry it on to completion until the day of Christ Jesus."

—Mark Lowry

Now that was written by the same little boy who was such a hyperactive child that he drove the teachers crazy. He did a pretty good job on us, too.

Again, I want to say, "Thank you Father, for letting us have the three children that You gave us. We are so grateful for that."

—Bev Lowry

Chapter Four
Mark of Achievement
(The Theater)

During 1966-67 things began to change when Mark had Mrs. Hollan for a teacher in the third grade. She cared for him in a genuine way. He knew it and I knew it. It was wonderful to think that someone really did care about what we were going through. It was hard on Mark, and it was also hard on me. This third grade teacher was a turning point in this eight-year-old child's life. God bless you, Mrs. Hollan!!!

There are some things about that time in our lives that I wish I had done differently. The truth is that I was only thirty-two myself. I hadn't attended college and studied Child development. I didn't know what was going on in his life. I thought that he should be able to understand that he had to be good. He had to do what we told him to do. I did not know that children can't think like we can. They have to mature to a certain place before they can understand like we do. I know that some Christians will say, "Oh, you can make them understand." What will work for one may not work the same for others. We must study our children and see what will work for them. Before you criticize some of the young parents in your church who are struggling with a hyperactive child, walk a day in their shoes.

The apostle Paul said, "When I was a child I thought as a child. But now I have put away childish things." I Cor. 13:11.

Isn't he saying there that children think differently than adults? He is. Jean Piaget came along years later and has shown that children do indeed have to mature and grow before they can understand as an adult can. But how many times did I tell my children, "I am going to tell you one time." No, I found, as a Mother, that I had to tell them many, many times. And sometimes I would have to tell them again.

I wish that as a young Mother I could have known this. I also wish that I would have looked through their eyes to see how they saw the situation. I really don't remember ever doing that. Maybe I did on occasion, I hope so. But I really don't remember. I think parents would do well to try to understand how their child sees the situations that they are going through.

I am not saying here that I would not discipline. Oh yes, I would discipline. One of the problems in our country today is a lack of respect for authority. This comes from a lack of discipline. Fifty years ago, in our country, everyone disciplined the same way. Most people grew up to love their parents, respect authority and obey the law. Today psychologists are saying that all physical punishment is wrong because some people will abuse their children. Abuse will never be done away within our society. Even if corporal punishment is outlawed in our country, abusive parents will still abuse. Making it unlawful for parents to spank their children will only lead to more lack of authority and respect for the laws of society. "Foolishness is bound in the heart of a child; but the rod of correction will drive it far from him." Prov. 22:15. However, I do believe in punishment that fits the offense for proper correction and teaching the child why he or she should not do a certain thing. Also, I do not believe in punishment when you are angry. We must 'rightly divide the Word of Truth'. II Tim 2:15. We are to discipline our children so that they will become disciples of Jesus Christ and so that they will know that we love them. The Bible says, "Whom the Lord loves He disciplines". If you sin and sin and sin and God doesn't discipline you, you're not in the family. We show love by discipline. But we better not abuse. We can discipline without abusing. And we must. Taking away a parents' God given right to discipline their child will not stop child abuse and will take children away from God.

I mentioned earlier that Mrs. Hollan let Mark "star" in the musical that she wrote. I believe that she was working on his self-esteem. She was trying to build into him some competency. Something that he could do that no one else in our family could do. Alfred Adler, the noted psychologist, says that children will mark their own territory when they come into a family. They generally will not do what the older siblings do, unless it is a family value. In other words, if the Mother and Father are involved, then all of the children will follow. We see that happen many times in sports, academics and music. If Mama and Daddy both watch Monday night football, the children may all be athletic. If Mama and Daddy turn off the TV and read, all of the children may be academic. They will turn off the TV, too, and read books. If Mama and Daddy both sing or play a musical instrument, the children will all be musical. This doesn't always happen, but most of the time it does. Children model their parents and do what they see them do. However, Adler said that if it's not a family value, the children will all mark their own territory. If one is athletic, the second may be athletic. The third may be musical, etc. The last one will be the best at something, even if it is being bad or a clown.

Mark was finding his own niche. And marking his territory.

We already knew that he could sing.

Mike and Mark both talked very early. It seemed that they were born talking, in sentences. Mike also sang on pitch very early. This thrilled me because I play the piano and sing. Charles says that he cannot carry a tune in a bucket but he plays the radio. I think that he really could but is convinced that he can't and doesn't. Anyway, Mark did not carry a tune early. In fact, when he was about three he came out of the nursery at church one day and was singing away. The only problem was that he knew all of the words to the songs but couldn't carry a tune. I remember saying to Charles, "This kid will never sing." Bite my tongue. I'm glad he didn't hear me. That could have become a self-fulfilling prophecy, and look what we would have missed!

By the age of four, he was standing on a chair in church singing solos.

He would sing in a little child's voice at church. At home he sang in a booming adult voice. We would beg him to sing in his 'big' voice. But he wouldn't. We even offered to pay him if he would sing in his big voice. Still no luck.

We went to a Davis family reunion, on my side of the family, when he was five. My Dad's family, all sang and played instruments. We gathered around the piano and sang old hymns. Mark got carried away and sang out in his big voice. The adults were shocked and applauded for him.

Well, you can imagine the rest. He was hooked. He sang in his big voice from then on. The people at our church loved it. He would sing on Sunday and later that night we would be taking his clothes off for bedtime and coins would fall out of his pockets. The little old ladies at our church would fill his pockets with change. He learned early that people liked his singing.

Then at the age of eight, in 1966, Mrs. Hollan was encouraging his singing and helping him feel that he was special.

Howdy Doody was the name of a children's TV show in Houston. We decided to let him try out for the show. He made it. So every once in awhile they would call him and let him sing on the show.

While doing that show he met other children. Some who danced or sang or played musical instruments. One of the Mothers there suggested to me that we should take Mark and let him try out for a part in one of the musicals offered at the Houston Music Theater. Every Fall they put on professional theater. The tryouts were in the Spring.

Charles and I decided to let him try out.

I was expecting Melissa in August of 1967, but I took Mark down to the theater to try out.

He loved to imitate Louis Armstrong with the scratchy voice. So he learned "Hello Dolly". I accompanied him at the piano.

We sat in the theater that Saturday morning watching the adults and teenagers try out. A director from New York was there to judge the tryouts. Most of the people would begin to sing and by the second line of the song the director would say, "Thank you very much, next?" He did this with almost everyone. He explained that this wasn't to be considered bad or that anything was wrong. He just knew when he had heard enough and he would call back the ones he was interested in. I really think it was done because of the time element.

When I saw what was happening I told Mark to sing only a little bit in Louie Armstrong imitation and then sing in his own voice because they would probably cut him off too. I wanted them to hear his own voice.

Finally his name was called. We went on stage and I took my place at the piano. And Mark began. They never stopped him. When he finished, the auditorium broke into applause. The director said, "Can you raise the key up some so I can hear his range?" I was shaking all over from nerves but Mark was cool as a cucumber. "No sir," I said. "I can't transpose that easily, but we'll be glad for one of the other accompanist, to help us out." One of the professional accompanists came to the stage. He raised Mark's key two or three times. Mark never missed a lick. He sang and each time the others applauded him. They said they would call him back.

One day in August, just after Melissa was born, the theater called to ask if Mark could come back and try out for a part in "Gypsy." Now I didn't know very much about the theater, but I did know "Gypsy" was about the stripper Gypsy Rose Lee. I very politely told the lady we really wouldn't be interested in Mark appearing in Gypsy, but we would be very happy to let him try out for "The Music Man" when it came up for tryouts. I thanked her for calling.

Sure enough, when the tryouts started for "The Music Man" we got a call from the Houston Music

Theater. I taught Mark one of the songs from the show and on a Saturday morning I took him out to the theater for tryouts.

I have never seen so many children in one place. There were boys and girls of all sizes and shapes. They read and sang and then they did call backs. By afternoon they were down to two or three boys. Then finally they chose Mark. They had to read the lines. "Thister, Thister, ----. He read it like he had been lisping all of his life.

Then they began choosing the girl. Finally they were down to two girls and the director asked Mark, "Which one do you want?" I held my breath. I really did not want Mark to answer. And he only said, "It really doesn't matter to me, sir." My, was I proud. Such manners on such a little boy! And he hadn't chosen either one.

When the choices had been made the director told me privately that Mark had the part the minute he opened his mouth. "Oh," I said, "I wish you had told me that." "Well, I could have, but I didn't know what to do with all the other mothers."

Mark loved the part of "Winthrop." Hal March played the part of "Professor Harold Hill" and Susan Watson played "Miriam, the Librarian."

When this show began Melissa was three months old. It was really a job getting him to the rehearsals and shows with such a small baby. Charles and Mike both helped a lot.

I was always there because I was afraid to ever leave him there without me. All of my life I had heard stories about the dangers of the theater. As I watched Mark's love for the theater grow, I asked Charles many times about my fears. "What if he really loves it and wants to go on with it?" "Don't worry," he would tell me, "we will control the situation."

As I walked out of church one Wednesday evening, the Pastor was standing at the door. I asked him, "Well, what do you think about Mark performing in the plays at the Houston Music Theater?"

He said, "Time will tell."

Well, time has told. That Pastor divorced his wife, and ran off with the Church Secretary. Since that time, I have been informed that he has converted to Judaism and is living in Israel.

Tommy Tune choreographed the show. He flew in from New York and stayed until the night before opening. One day he sat down by me in the back of the theater. "Mrs. Lowry, you have a very talented little boy. I have worked with many children and I can tell you that if he was in New York, he could play Broadway right now. I don't believe you and your husband are ready to move, but, you really should let him continue by taking him to a children's drama teacher here in Houston."

Tommy Tune scared me, but I trusted that Charles and I would be able to handle this.

The show ran for sixteen performances, every night except Monday night. Mark had a ball. One night the producer came up to me and said, "Mark is amazing. Every night is like opening night to him. He is fresh all the time."

All of the songs started cold. No introduction or anything. When the songs would start you would hear the xylophone bells in the background. It would pull the soloist up on key and then the live orchestra would join in. Mark's only solo was "Gary Indiana." Not one time did he start off key. The orchestra leader said, "The only one with perfect pitch is the kid. He always starts on key."

Every night after the show Hal March would come on stage and talk to the audience. He would always say something nice about Mark to the audience. Things like: "That kid makes me sick, he has four lungs."

Mark did love the theater and it was evident. The Houston Music Theater was in the round and he really did get a lot of training there.

They called him again for "Annie Get Your Gun" with Kay Starr. He got the role of "Little Jake," Annie's little brother. He had another grand time, and when the play's run was over in Houston, Kay Starr gave Mark a little toy pop-gun and I still have it. Years later, Mark renewed his acquaintance with Kay Starr and he visits her when he is in her area.

We let him enroll in the Children's Theater in Houston. We would take him out there once a week for lessons and he enjoyed the classes.

They put on plays for the parents. I think that was the first indication we had as a family that Mark could make people laugh. I remember a play they put on one time and his part was so funny that Charles, Mike and I laughed until the tears literally rolled down our cheeks. Well, at least Mike and I did. Charles laughed, but we really laughed.

He played the lead role in "Pinocchio." He was so good.

I remember one night that they wanted to teach Pinocchio to dance. I sat in the theater and didn't say anything. On the way home Mark said, "Mama, why didn't you tell them that I couldn't dance." I said, "Mark, it's only a show." "Well," he said, "you can't sit on the gate." He meant, "You can't straddle the fence." He was bothered by the fact that they wanted him to dance and he didn't believe in dancing. I said, "Let's wait and show it to Daddy and see what he says." When we got home Mark showed his Dad the little dance. Charles said, "It looks like a puppet to me." So Mark did the dance in the show and nothing else was said about it.

The teacher at the theater called me in one day and told me something that really startled me. "Mrs. Lowry, Mark has a sense of timing that you can't teach anyone. You either have it or you don't. I have only taught one other person who had that sense of timing. It was my own son and he is in London today studying for the stage. Mark has that kind of ability. I hope you will let him continue here with me." I was so shocked and a little frightened at the same time. I knew he had talent but to have someone else, especially his teacher, say so was really a little scary. You see, I didn't mind him being in the plays because we had definitely seen him settling down. He had found his niche. The people at the theater appreciated his talent and didn't mind his hyperactivity. They more or less accepted it as part of the package. I tried to talk to Mark's teacher about my fears. I told her that I wanted Mark to use his talent for God. I asked her if we could pick and choose the parts that he played. And would he be able to do that as he grew older. She said, "Yes, but it would be hard." I told her that I had seen people cry when Mark sang "How Great Thou Art" and that I would never want them to see him in a play on Saturday night that would cause his ministry on Sunday morning to have less effect. This might seem a little strange to some ears now that we are in the twenty-first century, but in the sixties there weren't very many outspoken Christians in the theater. We did not want Mark to end up in the theater and more importantly, we did not feel that God did either.

I went home and told Charles everything that she had said. I was really afraid that we had let him taste of something that we might really be sorry for later. Understand that all of this time we were very involved in our Church, Berean Baptist Church, Houston, Texas. Charles was a deacon and Sunday school teacher. I sang and played the piano for services.

So we began to pray in earnest, like we had not prayed before. We asked God to open up a way that Mark could "entertain" for Him. We had no idea of what we were asking. We just wanted help for our hyperactive son. We wanted Mark to serve the Lord and not the devil.

We moved to Spring, Texas, just north of Houston, in 1970 and enrolled him in the sixth grade in Spring Junior High School. During this time he was still going to the drama lessons and still trying out for parts.

One day we got a call from the Houston Grand Opera. They were looking for a child to play a part in "Johnny Schicci." It wasn't a big part but they had tried out many children for the part and didn't feel that they had the right one. Someone mentioned Mark and asked, "Why don't you try to find the little boy who played "Winthrop" in "The Music Man." So the Houston Music Theater gave them our number. We took him to the theater and he got the part on the spot.

It was great fun. It was totally different from the other theater. The stage wasn't in the round. It was at Jones Hall in Houston. (Little did we know that he would perform at Jones Hall as an adult with the Gaithers.)

When the Opera opened, Mark's whole school went in school busses to see him. He became quite a "little celebrity" at school. We were so proud of him. He was controlling his behavior better all the time. As his competency grew, his behavior improved.

Then the Music Theater called in children to try out for "Oliver." They didn't call in the children from their drama classes until they had tried out the children from the other school downtown and anyone else who wanted to try. I taught Mark the song, "Where is Love?" When the day came for the tryouts for the drama classes, his teacher was sitting beside the director. This was a new director from New York. He looked a little tired from watching so many children perform. The next boy to try out was trying for the role of "Jogger." The boy had taken dancing for years and really was good. The director knew that he had found his "Jogger." When Mark stood up next to try out for "Oliver" the director said, "Do you really want to try out after that?" Mark very quietly said, "Yes, sir." Mark began, "Where ----is love?" The directors' mouth opened in unbelief. After hearing all of those children, he had found both of the children's parts at the same time. I saw the children's drama teacher hand the director Mark's resume and pictures from the other plays. Oliver and Jogger were chosen.

We were excited for him to play the part of Oliver. It is such a cute story. It really would be good, clean, family entertainment.

This is the same time, remember, that Charles and I were praying that God would open a way for Mark to "entertain" for Him.

About this time Duke Westover, a long time family friend, called our house. He traveled the country building church buildings for various churches. Duke said, "I talked to J. G. Whitfield the other day. He is going to promote the first International Song Festival in Nashville in June 1970. I told him about Mark and he said to bring him to Nashville and he would put him on the program." I told Duke about the play "Oliver" and really did not think we would be able to go to Nashville because the time for "Oliver" and the song Festival would conflict. I thanked him anyway.

The next thing I heard was that "Oliver" had been canceled because of lack of funds. In fact all of the shows were canceled for that season because of lack of funds.

I called Duke and told him that we could go to Nashville after all.

We hadn't been going to gospel music concerts because we were so busy doing other things. Charles and I were both very active in our church. Mike was busy in little league football and Mark was in drama at the Houston Music Theater. Our Melissa was about two-and-one-half at this time. There are only so many hours in a day. But with this new opportunity, I believed that God was answering our prayers.

We took Mark to the Houston Music Hall to see a Gospel Concert. I knew that when he saw the singers perform, he would know how to work the stage. I was right. I don't remember all of the groups there that night, but I do remember one, "The Rambos." We sat in the balcony during the first part of the program and Mark loved it. He kept punching me in the ribs asking, "Why haven't we been coming to these?" "Because we haven't had time," I replied.

At intermission he asked Duke Westover if he could sit in one of his front row seats. Duke said, "Yes," and Mark got down as close as he could to the stage and fell in love with Reba Rambo. She was eighteen and he was eleven. Of course, he loved Dottie and Buck too.

It was easy to get him to learn the medley of songs that I prepared for him because he was so excited about going to Nashville and getting on that stage.

The medley started with "America the Beautiful," "This Land is Your Land'" and ending with "God Bless America." We bought him a blue suit, red shirt, white tie and white shoes. He looked so cute and very patriotic.

We headed for Nashville and a family vacation.

When we got there Duke was a little nervous. "Listen," he said, "those groups are fighting for time on the stage. They can only sing two songs. I am really afraid that you have come so far and Mark might not get on the stage."

"Don't worry, Duke," I said, "if nothing else we have had a great vacation and this is our first time in Nashville." I knew how we had prayed and I couldn't help but believe that God was answering our prayers.

That afternoon we were wandering around the arena while the singing was going on. Duke walked up to Mr. Whitfield to tell him that Mark was there. Just as he spoke to Mr. Whitfield, Mark appeared and Duke said, "Mr. Whitfield, I'd like you to meet Mark Lowry." Mark held out his hand to Mr. Whitfield and said, "I'm glad to meet you, Mr. Whitfield, and I sure do appreciate you letting me sing on your program tonight." Duke was shocked. But Mr. Whitfield, being the great man he is, said, "I'm glad you could come, Mark." Mark went on that night at nine o'clock. Prime time. We couldn't have asked for a better time. That program went on until the wee hours of the morning and Mark went on at nine o'clock. I knew that God was working in this.

When they called his name, he bounced onto the stage. And he began, "Oh beautiful, for spacious skies, for amber waves of grain. For purple mountains majesties above the fruited plain." The crowd was on their feet. I cried. Charles beamed and took pictures. Mike was so proud of his little brother.

When the song was over, I rushed backstage where Mark would be coming down the steps from the stage. He was already down and was standing, looking up at his idol, Reba Rambo. She was about two feet taller than he was and was looking down at him as she hugged him. She asked him if he had a record out. He said no and she said that she was sure that he would soon. Mark sure had a big grin on his face as he talked to Reba.

After the program many people from Booking Agencies and Recording Companies came around to talk to us. One of those was Lou Hildreth from Skylight Talent Agency. She said that she would like to book Mark on the road. We were also contacted by Bob MacKenzie of Benson Records who said they would like to sign Mark to a recording contract.

We ended up spending three additional days in Nashville talking to different agencies and recording companies and finally signing a booking contract and recording contract.

Mark made his first record for the Benson Company's "Impact Label" and Bob McKenzie arranged for the London Symphony Orchestra to play the music on his first professional album. Skylight Talent Agency, through Lou Hildreth, booked Mark on weekends in Saturday night gospel concerts. He was graciously backed by Gordon Jensen and the Orrells.

This began a great time of fun for us as a family. But also a time of learning and growing and trusting more than ever for the Will of the Lord for Mark's life as well as our own.

Mark was able to "entertain" for the Lord. Charles and I knew that God had answered our prayers.

When we returned to Houston, I called the drama teacher and told her what had happened.

She understood because of our previous conversation. She still wanted Mark to come to the theater for lessons and parts in plays. She said, "Please don't take him away from us." But, I knew that time would not permit it. She did too.

Little did we know how the events of that summer would change our lives.

Charles bought the 4104 GMC traveling bus of the Inspirations. The Inspirations were very helpful to Mark and us. Martin Cook and Archie Watkins gave us great insight to the Gospel Music Industry.

The next summer that bus was all over the South and Eastern coast, from Texas to Louisiana, Mississippi, Alabama, Florida, Georgia, South Carolina, North Carolina, Tennessee and Virginia.

We assembled a back-up group for Mark called the "Impacts." They played musical instruments and sang with Mark.

Charles would leave his law office on Friday afternoon, come home and we would load up the bus. It had nine bunk beds and a restroom.

Little four year old Melissa would walk on the bus, in Houston at 5 P.M. and later go to sleep in her bed and get off the bus the next morning in Nashville, as though it was just a routine trip.

Mike talked his Dad into letting him take his Honda Trail Bike in one of the bus' luggage bays. Mike rode that Honda in many a city that summer.

Thirteen year old Mark asked his Dad if he could sign the checks paid to the group of young men who made up the "Impacts," and his Dad allowed him to do so.

On one occasion, two of the young men in the "Impacts," both about nineteen or twenty years of age, made an appointment to see Charles in his law office. They told him that they resented thirteen-year-old Mark telling them that he paid their salaries. Charles told them, "That is exactly what he is doing." Those two young men got along with Mark a lot better after that visit.

*9-year-old Mark talking to "Marion the Librarian"
with "Professor Harold Hill" watching*

ART WALLACE

Broadway theatre-goers will recognize Art Wallace from last year's City Center revival of The Music Man, Talent '64, and Nowhere To Go But Up. Off-Broadway, he has either starred or been featured in Flahooley, The Tattooed Countes, The Golden Apple, and last season's Hotel Passionato. In touring companies of everything from Rigoletto to The Music Man, he has performed in over 200 cities in 44 states, plus a three-month tour of Europe in Kiss Me Kate while stationed there in 1958 with the 8th Infantry Division. Although primarily a stage actor, he has appeared on Television in Carmen, O'Halloran's Luck, The Morty Gunty Show, and Kaleidescope IV.

J. FRANK LUCAS

Mr. J. Frank Lucas will be remembered for his appearances this past summer at the Houston Music Theatre with John Raitt, Andy Devine, Gisele MacKenzie, Van Johnson, Patrice Munsel and Gardner McKay. During the course of his career he has appeared with many other stars including Miss Tallulah Bankhead, Groucho Marx, Richard Chamberlain, Ann Sothern, Linda Darnell, Tony Randall and Pat O'Brien and has appeared on television in Time for Elizabeth with Groucho Marx, on the Bob Hope Chrysler Theatre and is currently to be seen world wide in a featured role in the 20th Century Fox film Curse of the Living Corpse.

LESSLIE NICOL

Lesslie Nicol completed a successful seven months run, in June of this year, as the Innkeepers Wife in the Off-Broadway musical hit Man With a Load of Mischief. Since then she has been making T.V. Commercials. In 1964 she played Mrs. Pearce in My Fair Lady with the late Zachary Scott and again in 1966 with Dorothy Collins, Anita Gillette and Michael Allinson, and in 1965 played in The Music Man with Gig Young. Miss Nicol has been seen as Mrs. Elliot in Epitaph for George Dillon, Mrs. Bramson in Might Must Fall, Rebecca Nurse in The Crucible, and in many leading character roles of Gilbert & Sullivan Operettas and English Musical Comedies.

MARK LOWRY

STEVE STEPHENSON

A versatile performer who divides his time between the stage and night clubs. Considered one of the top Singing-Pianists on New York's night club scene, he has just completed another successful engagement Downstairs at the Duplex in Greenwich Village, a club that has become synonymous with his name. Listed with "The Tar Heel Who's Who", he began his acting career in his native North Carolina where he was featured in Paul Green's outdoor drama The Lost Colony. His many credits include Off-Broadway's hit musical Hamlet of Stepney Green, and several seasons with musical tents.

90

Review of "The Music Man" production by the Houston Music Theatre, November 1967

On November 15, 1967, D. J. Hobdy, a Chronicle reporter in Houston, Texas, wrote a review about the musical "The Music Man." He gave a good reveiw of Choreographer Tommy Tune and his tireless chorus.

He also reviewed the talents of Hal March as "Professor Harold Hill" and Susan Watson as "Marion the Librarian."

Then he said, "And if all the Houston Music Theatre troupers had the projection and charm of 9-year-old Mark Lowry, as the "Lisping Wintrophy" turned on by a trumpet, rapport could be almost immediate."

Mike, age 12, Melissa, age 18 months,
and Mark, age 10

Mark with Kay Starr in "Annie Get Your Gun"

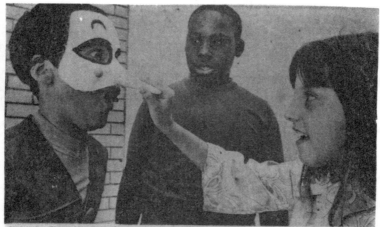

DRAMATIC TOUCH

Some 300 Houston public school youngsters got a first-hand experience with drama today when Focus on Achievement youngsters saw a performance of "Pinnochio" at the Houston Music Theater, then went backstage to meet the actors. Pinnochio gets his nose checked by Dezerderry Brown, 8, of 5104 Schuler, as 9-year-old Gregory Mims, 5232 Blossom, observes. The actor is 12-year-old Mark Lowry, 17403 Anvil. FOA is financed by the federal government as a summer enrichment program.

1970

Mark Lowry, 12, son of Mr and Mrs Charles G. Lowry of Spring, plays the title role in "Pinocchio," the Houston Music Theatre's Studio VII production of the enchanting fairy tale. It opens Saturday and will be performed eac⁺ Saturday through June a⁺ PM, with a 7:30 PM June 18.

93

Skylite Talent, Inc.

1516 HAWKINS ST.
NASHVILLE, TENN. 37202
(615) 244-6116

Mrs. Lou Wills Hildreth, Director

J. G. WHITFIELD, Chairman of the Board

LLOYD ORRELL, Pres.

JOEL GENTRY, Executive Vice-Pres.

W. B. NOWLIN, Vice-Pres. and Treas.

THE ORRELLS

THE INSPIRATIONS

MARK LOWRY

SAMMY HALL SINGERS

*The Benson Music
Company's Bob McKenzie
and wife, Joy*

Portions of an Article in the Houston Chronicle after Mark's performance singing on New Year's Eve, 1970, at a Fund Raising Event for the cure of Cystic Fibrosis

Morris Frank, reporter for the Houston Chronicle wrote an article titled "Of Cabbages and Kings, Mark Lowry, 12, Sings Like Bell"

"What with last night being New Year's Eve maybe we have bells on the mind.

Anyway, we are thinking how this 12-year-old youngster, Mark Lowry sings like a bell.

With all others who heard him at the Cystic Fibrosis Golf Tournament banquet at the Marriott, we were tremendously impressed.

The youngster, son of attorney and Mrs. Charles G. Lowry, is a seventh grader at Spring Middle School.

Mark not only has a fine voice, he has an album out, "I'm The Least In The Kingdom," but he has the poise of an adult. Indeed he has much more poise in front of a mike than lots of adults.

His charming mother accompanied Mark.

With a Yuletide dance with conflicting music slated in the next room for later in the evening, Mark was brought on while the food was being served in the interest of time.

However, the youngster, who has been singing since he was four, was unruffled as if he were in the chorus of a Christmas program at Spring Middle School.

The dynamic University of Houston golf coach, Dave Williams, who is always on the lookout for talent, golf or otherwise, heard Mark at a previous banquet.-----.

A grand evening kicked off with the ringing of the singing of the bells by the undaunted young man from Spring School, Mark Lowry."

Singer Mark Lowry

12-Year-Old Singer Cuts Album Here

By GIL ROWLAND

Mark Lowry, who began singing at the age of 4, is in Greenville to record a new album at Mark V Studio.

The 12-year-old musician spent four hours yesterday and was scheduled for a similar session today putting 15 gospel songs on tape.

Bill Westover, his manager, said 10 of the numbers will go on the record.

Lowry's first album for Heartwarming Records was "I'm the Least in the Kingdom."

The boy's mother, Mrs. Beverly Lowry, is a musician on the staff of the Berean Baptist Church in Houston. Mark began singing in the church when he had to stand on a chair to reach the microphone.

He sang in several Broadway musicals in Houston. Last July he was invited to sing in an international contest in Nasvhille.

Since that time he, his mother, and his back-up group have traveled over 35,000 miles doing concerts.

He attends school an average of three days a week, and his teachers allow him to make up his other work. He will take a correspondence course this summer while traveling.

13-year-old Mark and baby sister, Melissa,
visit Parrot Jungle in Florida

Union Baptist Association

Mark Lowry To Perform At Northshore

Mark Lowry

Much is said today about the younger generation of our nation. We hear many reports about campus riots, violence and disrespect for authority. Sunday, January 14th, 1973, at 7:00 p.m. we offer you the opportunity to hear a different story of today's youth. Fourteen year old **Mark Lowry** of Houston, Texas, will be with us to sing and give his views and ideas of what a young person can and should expect from living in the last half of the 20th Century. Mark Lowry is an accomplished singer with four long playing albums to his credit. Mark is a Heartwarming recording artist and has appeared on national television and sung in concerts and churches all across America. We, of Northshore Baptist Church, 6511 Uvalde Rd., Houston, Texas, invite you to come and hear this remarkable young man. We know that you will be glad that you did.

Mark Lowry

14 years old

Sings Gospel Music all over the U.S.A. in concerts, churches, revivals and youth activities.

Has his own radio program on KFMK-FM in Houston, Texas at 6 p.m. every Saturday.

Is booked through Skylite Talent Agency in Nashville, Tennessee.

Has two HEART WARMING albums entitled "I'm the Least In The Kindgom" and "I'd Rather Have Jesus".

Chapter Five
Remarkable Miracle
(The Wreck)

In 1975, at the age of seventeen, Mark started to college at Lynchburg Baptist College in Lynchburg, Virginia. Mark had obtained a music scholarship from a college in Florida, however, he wanted to go to college where his brother, Mike, was enrolled and completed his freshman year in 1974.

We were busy raising our daughter, Melissa, and the two boys were 1,300 miles away in college. They were calling and writing us and coming home for various holidays. The next three years were fairly routine.

Then alarming news came. I will never forget March 17, 1978. Early that morning I heard "Ring –Ring – Ring!!!!" The telephone rang insistently. I hurried from the bathroom to answer. "Hello," I said, a little impatiently. I was late for my beauty shop appointment already and wasn't anxious to get tied up on the phone.

"Mrs. Lowry? I'm Virginia Smith, a nurse at Carlisle Hospital in Carlisle, Pennsylvania. Your son, Mark, has been in an accident."

Stunned, I said, "How is he?"

"Well," she continued, "he has a broken leg and will be tied up for a few days." I sat down on the bed. "How are the others?" I asked.

"Two of them are in intensive care and one is in surgery," she replied.

"Who is in surgery and how bad are they hurt?" I could hardly get my breath or think.

"Charles Hughes is in surgery with a head injury," Mrs. Smith said.

I felt as if the blood had drained from my body, but I began to understand that this was very serious. "Please give me your name again and tell me how I can call you back." I reached for a pencil and all I could find was a black crayon, but I used it anyway.

"My name is Virginia Smith at Carlisle Hospital in Carlisle, Pennsylvania," and she gave me the hospital phone number. My hand was shaking so badly that I could hardly write. She continued, "Mark gave me your number and asked me to call you."

I felt relieved a little bit to know that Mark was able to give her this information.

"Mrs. Lowry, we don't know anything about the other boys. Can you tell us a little bit about them?"

"The boys are from Lynchburg Baptist College in Lynchburg, Virginia. They are an evangelistic team that travels out of that school." I was shaking so badly. I told her, "I will call you back shortly."

I hung up the phone and ran into the den. Don't ask me why I changed phones. I just needed to run. I had a tremendous surge of energy. Charles, my husband, had left earlier to take our daughter, Melissa, to school. I called his office and left word for him to call me. I told his secretary about the accident. I called Mike, our other son at his apartment in Lynchburg. His roommate answered the phone. He told me, "Mike is in class, but I'll go get him."

"Can you tell me how to call Dr. Falwell please?" I asked. "Yes, Mrs. Lowry," and he gave me Thomas Road Baptist Church's phone number. I put the receiver down and picked it up again and dialed the number he gave me. The switchboard operator said, "Thomas Road Baptist Church."

My voice shook uncontrollably as I said, "Please, I need to talk to Dr. Falwell immediately." The next voice I heard said, "This is Dr. Falwell's office, Jeannette Hogan speaking."

I replied, "Mrs. Hogan, this is Beverly Lowry. Mark and Charles Hughes have been in a bad wreck up in Carlisle, Pennsylvania. I need to talk to Dr. Falwell." Her reply was, "I'm sorry, Mrs. Lowry, he is in a meeting in Holland, Michigan. I will get word to him. Give me your phone number."

As I gave her my number, I could hardly believe this was happening. I felt that I was dreaming and I wanted very much to wake up. These boys were out doing what God called them to do. My thinking was very fuzzy.

As I put the phone back on the hook, I heard Charles coming through the door. I wanted to just fall on him and cry. He said very calmly, "Now Beverly, don't get excited. Let's find out what's happened."

He called Virginia Smith at Carlisle Hospital. She told Charles the same thing that she had told me earlier. She told him that Mark was sedated and that we could talk to him in about two hours. Two hours!! That seemed like an eternity.

"Now, Beverly, I want you to go to your beauty salon appointment. Then come to the office and we'll call Mark. We'll put him on a plane and bring him home." Charles said this so calmly I believed that it would be that simple.

Beauty shop appointment! Did he say beauty shop appointment? How could I ever go? But, he insisted, so I did keep the appointment. As I walked out the door, the sun was shining so bright. The day was beautiful. Spring was everywhere and the birds were singing. My heart was so heavy that I could hardly believe the birds would want to sing. As I sat under the dryer, all I could do was pray and cry. The thoughts were running through my mind. I think I remembered Mark's whole life in that short hour. He was special even before birth.

I didn't want him to go through this by himself. Mark was nineteen years old and attending Lynchburg Baptist College in Lynchburg, Virginia, thirteen hundred miles from Houston, Texas, where we lived. We moved back inside of Houston while the two boys were in college.

He was traveling with three other students in an evangelistic team. In the wee hours of the morning of March 17, 1978, the van in which they were traveling skidded on a patch of ice about five miles south of Carlisle, Pennsylvania. The van struck the guardrail on the right side of the road and then skidded back into the middle of the road and was hit broadside by a Mack truck.

Later I was to find out that Charles Hughes had head injuries and would be in a coma for ten weeks. Dick Bernier had broken ribs. David Musselman had battered and broken ribs. Mark had a dislocated shoulder, eleven broken bones, including one leg, both ankles and a complication of broken bones called Fat Embolism. He was really sick and within 24 hours after the accident he would be in serious condition and he would almost die.

The whole week before the wreck I had been sewing and listening to Manley Beasley's tapes on faith. Many years later I had the opportunity to tell Manley that I wasn't going to listen to his tapes on faith anymore because every time I heard him speak on it, God called on me to live it. I was just kidding.

When I went to get my ticket to Carlisle, I was told that the plane was sold out from Houston to Chicago and also from Chicago to Harrisburg. I exclaimed, "You don't understand, my son has been in an accident and I must get to him!" A lady stuck her head out from behind a partition and said, "We had a cancellation about 30 minutes ago. I don't know why we hadn't put it on the screen yet."

The girl waiting on me said, "Because it is her ticket."

I said, "Yes, it is."

So I went straight to Harrisburg, Pennsylvania, by way of Chicago, without a hitch. I told everyone on the plane where I was going. During that trip, I thought of Mary, the mother of Jesus. I was hurting very badly that day, but I know that Mary hurt so much more when she watched her perfect son being crucified. I arrived in Carlisle, Pennsylvania, at 10:30 PM. When I got to the hospital I leaned over my son's bed and said, "Mark, I wish I could trade places with you." Without a pause Mark said, "Mama, I don't want you to trade places with me, but I sure would like Madelyn Murray O'Hare to trade places with me." Even in pain he was trying to make us all laugh.

I stayed up all night. The next morning everyone was trying to make me go to bed. They were so nice, and were really trying to help...but one thing I learned is that when someone is going through this kind of intense emotion, it is better to leave them alone. God gives you so much strength and grace at that time. I was not even tired, but I was going to go to bed just to get them to leave me alone. At the time, I didn't think Mark was in any serious danger.

I was headed for the elevator when my son, Mike, who had come from Lynchburg, Virginia stepped off of it. We hugged each other in the hallway.

About that time the doctor walked up to me and said, "Mrs. Lowry, Mark has gone into a complication called Fat Embolism. It is a complication of breakage of the long bones of the legs. Fat leaks out of the bone marrow through the cracks in the bones and causes blockage of oxygen to the brain."

Then he said, "He will be mentally retarded or die." Stunned by this announcement, I said, "Doctor, I am from Houston, Texas, the medical center of the world. Do I need to move him or can you help him here? Money is no object."

The doctor said, "We are doing all that can be done here." I asked what they were doing for his condition and was told, "We are giving him heparin, cortisone, and oxygen." I said, "I don't know anything about Fat Embolism but I know he will be all right."

I called my husband in Houston and he called our bone doctor who was head of the orthopedic surgeons in Houston. The doctor told Charles that if that doctor found the Fat Embolism that fast he must be a good doctor. He said in Houston they would treat it with heparin, cortisone, and oxygen. Needless to say, this made us feel much better.

What we did not know until much later, the morning of the wreck, the staff of nurses and the doctors had their weekly early morning meeting in which they discussed different medical conditions and how to diagnose and treat them. That morning the subject was Fat Embolism. Within a few minutes after that meeting was over, one of the nurses called the orthopedic surgeon who was treating Mark, and told him she thought Mark had Fat Embolism. We believe that the Lord was involved in that meeting.

They put Mark in ICU. He was delirious. When they would tie his arms down to keep him from pulling the oxygen tube out of his nose, he would tell the doctor that he would be good and not pull it out. Then the minute the doctor untied his arms, out came the tube. So they had to keep him tied.

Mike made me go to the motel to spend the night. I did not sleep. I picked up my Bible to read. When I got to Psalm 27 verse 13, I was struck by it. "I had fainted, unless I had believed to see the goodness of the Lord in the land of the living." To me, that meant they were not going to die. I said, "Lord, You said the land of the living, not the land of the dying." They are going to live. And I never doubted it again. God said He would give us peace when we need it and I never had any peace when I thought of Mark or Charles dying. God was proving His love and watch care for us again.

The following morning as we returned to the hospital, I rode in the back seat with Kathy Hughes, Charles Hughes' wife. I started singing, "Promises," the song Mark and I had sung all over the country, the song that had helped me get through Melissa's ordeal with diabetes. The words to the song held a special meaning that morning. "He didn't promise my heart would not be broken, but He did say He'd mend it again." When I reached the hospital floor that Mark was on, I was met by Virginia Smith, the nurse who had called me in Houston to tell me about the wreck. She said, "Mrs. Lowry, we think Mark is out of the delirium. He seems normal, but we want you to come and talk to him and see what you think."

I bent over his bed and said, "Hi, Mark. You guys were on your way to a meeting in Tioga City, New York. But this morning your ministry is nationwide. People are praying for you everywhere." He said, "Mama, get my Bible and read the verses that are written on my cast." I started reading and he said, "Not just the verse, read the whole chapter." So I stood in ICU reading his Bible to him. The nurse on duty said, "That's a good boy you have there." I said, "Yes ma'am. How do you know that?" She said, "Because not one curse word has come out of his mouth. Usually when we have teenagers in here they are cursing and saying all kinds of horrible things. The only thing he has said is that he called me the wicked witch of the west. And he also wanted me to call his dumb mother."

She said, "I was on duty when they brought these boys into the emergency room. I knew that something was different about them. They were not screaming or cursing. The peace of God was so present in the emergency room that the doctors and nurses were whispering and speaking very softly to each other." Many of the attending nurses told us, "We will never be the same since these boys have come here."

We moved Mark to Houston the following week. We had to purchase three airline tickets, one for me and two for Mark, in order for his bed to be stretched over two seats. Upon arrival, I watched a little skinny ambulance driver and his little skinny female helper lift Mark off the plane and place him in the ambulance. I was afraid they would drop him, but they knew what they were doing and he arrived at our house without being dropped.

Mark was very pale and thin at this time. His accident was the main topic at our church and many other churches. People all over the country were praying for Mark, and the other young men with him in the accident, as a result of Dr. Jerry Falwell announcing the accident on The Old Time Gospel Hour television program and asking people to pray for them.

On April 10, 1978, I wrote the following letter to many of Mark's friends.

"Mark asked me to write this letter for him as he is still not feeling up to answering all of his mail.

There is no way that I can tell you what is in my heart. Each one of you who has written, called, visited or in some way expressed your love and concern for Mark, Charles, Dave and Dick, hold a special place in my heart. I thank you for the many prayers that you have offered for the boys and for the ones you'll continue to offer. We could not have come this far without them.

It is true that we have gone through a valley and it's certainly not our desire to pick a trial like this one. But God is faithful. He really manifests His love and concern for His children at a time like this. I praise Him for it.

As much as the boys travel, they could have been on a road without a hospital or doctors nearby. But God in His mercy allowed them to be on a highway within ten minutes of a great hospital with excellent doctors and an unbelievable nursing staff. The churches of all denominations opened their hearts and homes to help us in any way.

I believe that Jesus Christ was and is being glorified in it all.

When Mark was in ICU on Saturday night and Sunday, his nurse told me that she was called in to work at 6:30 A.M. on that Friday morning. (March 17). She said this, "Tell all the parents of those boys that I have worked in many emergency rooms. There is always screaming and cursing in an emergency room. But when I walked into that emergency room, the eight doctors and all the nurses were working quickly and quietly. There was no screaming and cursing from those boys. The peace of God was so present in that room that no one could deny it. As the boys would come to and go out again, they were cool and calm."

Oh how my heart rejoiced at those words. The Psalmist said, "When my father and my mother forsake me, then the Lord will gather me up." Psa. 27:10 There is a time when as a parent we are unable to comfort and protect our children, but it is such a blessing and comfort to know that as I slept in Houston, Texas, unaware of what my child was going through, that there is One Who neither slumbers nor sleeps, but Who carefully comforts His child in pain or sorrow. That's enough to make me shout.

As I traveled to Carlisle on that Friday, I thought of Mary and my heart was really moved to think how she must have felt as she stood at the foot of the cross and watched her beloved son crucified. I would imagine that if she could have she would have traded places with Him that day. But she could not, for she was not God.

When I arrived at the Hospital that night, Mark said, "Mama, a song keeps going over in my mind, 'Take the dearest thing to me, if that's how it must be, to draw me closer to You, Let the disappointments come, lonely days without the sun, if, if, if," I said, "If through sorrow more like You I'll become." He said, "NO Mama, no more of that more like You stuff. I want to be JUST LIKE HIM." There were several people around his bed. We almost had a shouting spell.

Another song that he kept repeating was a song by Rick and Rosemary Wilheim. It says, "God would not ask us to go where He would not lead. He is in control of things and that's good enough for me."

In the last three weeks many of the songs Mark sings have been going through my mind. It seems they all have a "new" meaning now.

We don't question our heavenly Father about this. We know that He knows what is happening and we trust Him completely. The last night before we left for Houston, I stood in the ICU room and talked to a couple of nurses. One said, "This hospital will never be the same because of those boys coming through here." Praise the Lord! Maybe God will use this team, Charles, Mark, Dave and Dick to bring a revival in Carlisle, Pennsylvania. That will sweep America. I have faith to believe that Charles Hughes will preach again. Oh how satan desires to destroy – But GOD still hears and answers prayers. Please keep praying. No matter how long it takes, please keep praying.

I'm sorry to have to send a duplicated letter like this but there is no way I could write each of you personally. You have been so good to write to us. When I see you, I'll hug your neck and thank you for your prayers and concern for all the boys.

The morning we left Carlisle to fly to Houston, Dr. Green came in to discharge us. He said, "Mark, you may get back this way before your cast comes off. You come on up here and I'll take it off for you." Mark said, "Well, Dr. Green I will come and see you, because I'd like for you to see me when I'm whole." Dr. Green said, "Mark, I have seen you at your very lowest and that's when you know if a person is whole or not."

We love the people of Carlisle, Pennsylvania. They will always be a permanent part in the ministry of Mark Lowry, Charles Hughes, Dave Musselman, and Dick Bernier.

Love, in Jesus,

Beverly Lowry"
(Mark's mom)

When I flew to Carlisle, Pennsylvania, Charles stayed in Houston, Texas and took care of our daughter, Melissa, who was in third grade in our Christian School, at Greenwood Village Baptist Church. Our pastor, Harold Clayton, told Melissa that her brother Mark was in an accident and had a dislocated shoulder.

When Melissa heard Brother Clayton tell her Mark had a dislocated shoulder, she started crying and asked, "Will they be able to find his shoulder?" She thought his shoulder was missing.

We moved to Lynchburg, Virginia in December 1978 and Charles and I traveled to Carlisle, Pennsylvania in the early part of 1979 and met Dr. Green and his lovely wife. We went to dinner with them and had a great visit.

Dr. Green and his family drove through a snow storm from Carlisle, Pennsylvania to Lynchburg, Virginia to watch Mark in his senior play at Liberty Baptist College (Now Liberty University). The play was "The Music Man." Mark played "Professor Harold Hill" and this was the same play in which he played "Lisping Winthrop" when he was nine years old in Houston, Texas.

Dr. Green told me he considered Mark a miracle. He said, "I thought surely he would die or be mentally retarded."

Mark has told this story in many of his concerts and says, "Well, I didn't die."

*Pictures of the wrecked van
and Mama visting Mark in the Hospital*

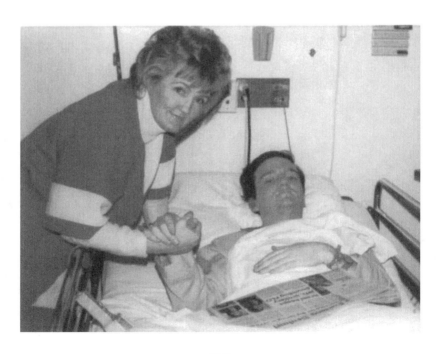

Excerpts from
an Article in the Evening Sentinel, Carlisle, Pennsylvania by Jeff Hawks, Staff Writer, which appeared Wednesday, March 22, 1978, five days after the wreck

Four evangelists found themselves in the Carlisle Hospital after their van was struck by a tractor-trailer.

Charles Hughes, 22, in critical condition. Richard G. Bernier, the 18-year-old driver, suffered bruises after the van he was driving hit a patch of ice two miles south of I-81's exit 12, and then hit broad side by the tractor-trailer.

Their survival from the high-speed collision evoked an outpouring of sympathy from admirers around the country.

The evangelists are associated with Thomas Road Baptist Church, Lynchburg, Virginia, home of the Old Time Gospel Hour television program.

Hundreds of calls from every state in the nation averaging about one every fifteen minutes over the weekend.

Jeff quoted David Musselman, 27, saying "They tell us they are praying for us."

Mark Lowry told the reporter, "I didn't know how many people cared about us."

Family and friends were in the hospitality room handling the calls on three phones as the switchboard transferred the calls.

Lowry thrown from the van, suffered a fractured leg, pelvis, rib and collarbone. He told the reporter, "our purpose is to tell people about a literal place called Hell. If we have to go through this to tell people about Hell, then this is worth it because it's like a vice squeezed it all together."

For Me To Live Is Christ
GOD'S WAY IS NOT
MAN'S WAY

By Charles Hughes

(As appeared in FAITH AFLAME MARCH-APRIL 1979)

It is clear to anyone who studies his Scripture and lives for God that God's way is not man's way. The Bible tells us in Isaiah 55:8, "For my thoughts are not your thoughts, neither are your ways my ways, saith the Lord."

The way to really live, to get the most out of life, is to die. Die to self and live for Christ. Take up your cross, deny self, and follow Him. Man says live it up, eat, drink, and be merry. God says to present your body a living sacrifice. In Galatians 2:20 Paul said, "I am crucified with Christ: nevertheless I live; yet not I, but Christ liveth in me and the life which I now live in the flesh I live by the faith of the Son of God, who loved me, and gave himself for me."

The way to really get the most out of life is to give. Man says you should get all you can. In Luke 6:38 God says, "Give, and it shall be given unto you...."

It is important that Christians take a stand. Leonard Ravenhill tells us that a man who fears God will fear no man. We read in Psalm 118:6, "The LORD is on my side: I will not fear: what can man do unto me?"

God's way to have real joy is to weep. Psalm 126: 5 tells us, "They that sow in tears shall reap in joy."

As Christians, we speak of "blind faith," God's way to have that blind faith, that faith that moves mountains, the evidence of things not seen, is by hearing the Word of God, Romans 10:17 tells us, "So then faith cometh by hearing, and hearing by the Word of God." Have you heard the Word of God today?

As 20th century Christians, there is much talk today of being filled with the Spirit. God's way of being filled with the Spirit is to be empty of self. Our lives should be void of selfish motives and goals.

We are in a great spiritual warfare against the devil. God's way to victory is surrender. If we surrender totally to God, we defeat the devil. If, as Christians, we live for self, the devil then gets the victory in our life. The question is, are you going to live for the Lord or for the devil?

Are you really living? Why not die to self? Are you really getting the most out of life? Why not give? Are you taking a stand? Why not kneel? Do you have real joy? Why not weep? Do you fear man? Why not fear God? Do you have blind faith, the kind that led Dr. Falwell to schedule a commencement speaker while he was unconscious in a coma, and had been for several weeks? Humanly speaking, as far as man was concerned, it would have been impossible for me to speak for commencement. But God says, "My thoughts are not your thoughts."

Are you filled with the Spirit? Are you empty of self? Do you have real victory, that peace that passeth all understanding, that joy unspeakable, that love unexplainable? Have you surrendered your all to Him? Why not go God's way, all the way, which is the only way to really live!

Another speaker now picks up here.

Not much laughter was heard around the ministries of the Thomas Road Baptist Church on March 17, 1978. A silent sadness and attitude of prayer pervaded all who had heard the news.

Charles Hughes and his team, members of the Jerry Falwell Evangelistic Association, had left Lynchburg at midnight. They were driving to New York to conduct a rally. Interstate 81 was icy, and as they ascended an incline at approximately 5 a.m., their van slid on the ice and was hit broadside by a semi-trailer descending the hill.

"All the boys are in critical condition," came the report. "Charles will not live through the day, they say."

Many could not help but picture vibrant, smiling Charles, a "fireball preacher" whose consuming desire in life was to see men come to a saving knowledge of Jesus Christ. In his senior year at Liberty Baptist College he had been chosen "Preacher of the Year." He now lay in a coma with massive brain-stem damage.

We waited and prayed. Time and again, day after day, Charles went to the very brink of death, and each time God saw fit to spare his life.

The other team members, Dave Musselman, Mark Lowry, and Richard Bernier began to improve and were dismissed from the hospital. And yet Charles remained in the coma.

Charles' wife and family would not give up hope. They ministered to the hospital personnel and prayed continually. Charles' father, Dr. Robert Hughes (Dean of Liberty Baptist Seminary), when told time and time again that Charles could only live a few minutes longer, would reply. "No, God has given me the assurance that Charles will preach again." Such deep faith is rarely seen in men today. People all over the nation continued steadfast in prayer while medical experts worked feverishly to save Charles' life.

Then one day, two and a half months after the accident, Charles miraculously came out of the coma.

He had received about 60 pints of blood and had undergone seven surgeries. No words could describe the reverberation in the auditorium of the Thomas Road Baptist Church the Sunday morning when, supported by his father, Charles walked slowly onto the platform. Thousands stood and cried and applauded. We could only breathe, "To God be all the glory."

Today, Charles is again attending Liberty Baptist Seminar. He is preaching and telling people with an urgent fervency that Jesus saves. This summer he will conduct 100 one-night rallies across the United States.

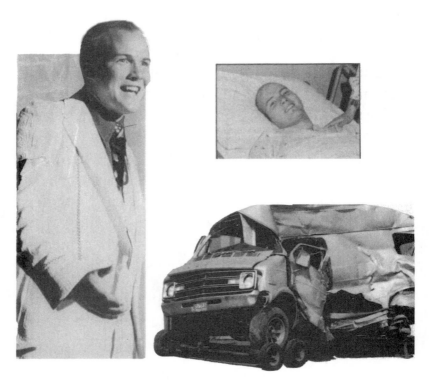

Charles Hughes preaching, in Hospital after coma, and the wrecked van

Chapter Six
A Mark of Revelation
(A Trip To Our Orthopedic Surgeon)

Charles took Mark to our family orthopedic surgeon, (We had a family orthopedic surgeon because Mike had broken several bones growing up).

Dr. Thomas Moore x-rayed Mark's chest, pelvis and legs. As he looked at the x-rays, with Charles and Mark looking on, he said, "Mark, both of your ankles are broken and you should not put any weight on either one of them. If you do, I will probably have to operate and put a pin in your ankle."

Mark had been told in Carlisle, he only had one broken ankle.

Mark told us all he could think about was the nurse in physical therapy, in Carlisle, telling him to walk to the end of the parallel bars and pivot on his good foot and him telling her he did not have a good foot. And he was right, they were both broken.

Each night, Charles helped Mark take a shower. He had casts on both legs, one leg from the pelvis to his toes, the other leg from his knee to his toes.

Have you ever tried to lift a 175-pound person with both legs in casts into a shower stall and then pick him up and place him in a wheel chair?

Charles told me one afternoon, as he came home from work, one of the ladies from our church had brought Mark a cake. As Charles entered Mark's bedroom, the lady was running a coat hanger wire up and down the inside of his leg cast, scratching his leg.

Mark was really getting royal treatment from the ladies of our church.

One of his Lynchburg Baptist College (now Liberty University) professors, Dr. A. T. Abraham, dropped by to visit Mark.

He told us he remembered one thing that was very unusual about both Mike and Mark, who were in his class.

He said one day the class was having a discussion about divorce in families and how this caused dysfunction in the home. He then told us Mike and Mark both told the class they could not relate to that because their parents were still married to each other and they had never heard their parents argue in front of them. (That does not mean we did not argue, just not in front of our children). That made us feel good.

Mark continued his recovery through the summer and announced to us that he would like to go back to college in Lynchburg, Virginia two weeks early. We bought Mike a new Pontiac Trans Am when he was a senior in college and promised Mark a new car for his senior year.

Chapter Seven
The Mark of a Senior College Student
(Mark's New Car)

In the summer of 1978, Mark and Charles drove to several car dealerships looking for a new car for Mark. They would park and Charles would help Mark get out of the car. He would stand up on two crutches and they would enter the showroom.

They visited the Chrysler Dealership, the Chevrolet Dealership and the Ford Dealership, all to no avail. Mark told his Daddy he did not see any car he liked.

Charles was encouraging him to purchase a four-door car. He told Charles the same thing Mike told him and later Melissa, "Four-door cars are for old people."

They then drove to the Mercury Dealership and as Mark got out of the car he said, "Daddy, I see my car."

Charles told me he looked in the direction Mark was pointing and prayed the car he saw was not the car Mark wanted.

It was a two door Cougar. Orange top, orange trunk and midnight blue everywhere else.

But that is the one he wanted, so that is the one he drove home that afternoon with casts on both legs.

Chapter Eight
Healing Mark
(Mark Returns To College)

In order to leave two weeks early for college, Mark convinced his orthopedic doctor in Houston that he would make an appointment with an orthopedic doctor when he returned to Lynchburg and have that doctor contact his Houston doctor.

His Houston doctor gave Mark permission to leave for Lynchburg. So, two weeks before school started in the fall of 1978, Mark pulled out of our driveway with two casts on his legs and his crutches and suitcases in the back seat.

Charles was concerned that he might be stopped as a suspected drug dealer driving that multi-colored Cougar, but to our relief he made the trip just fine. He stopped at several friend's houses on the way to Lynchburg.

We must admit that his Cougar was a very fine automobile and he kept it for several years.

He now drives a four-door car, and so does his brother, Mike, and sister, Melissa.

Pastor Harold Clayton (Greeenwood Village Baptist Church, Houston, Texas), Mark & Dad

Mark playing "Professor Harold Hill" in "The Music Man" in his Senior Year in College

Mark at the signing of a contract with the representatives of Word Music Company

Brother Mike, Mama and Mark

Mr. and Mrs. Charles Lowry
3937 Fort Ave.
Lynchburg, VA 24502

Bill Gaither

P.O. BOX 737 ALEXANDRIA, INDIANA 46001 • (317) 724-4441

Dear Ben & Char —

Thanks so much for your
kindness last weekend in Lynchburg.
The food & fellowship was fantastic!
We are really enjoying Mark. What
a great kid!

Blessings to you!

Your friends,
Bill & Gloria

131

Top right and next page: Mark singing with Mama in production of Mark Lowry on Broadway.
Bottom picture: sister Melissa, Dad, Mark & Mama

Top Right: Anthony Burger and Mark
Left: Mama and Mark
Center Right: Sandi Patty and Mark
Bottom Left: Bill Gaither Vocal Band
Bottom Right: Bill Gaither Vocal Band

133

Chapter Nine
A Remarkable Review
(Some incidents in the Life of Our Hyperactive Son)

We brought Mark home from the hospital five days after he was born because that was the customary length of time a new Mother spent in the hospital with her new-born in 1958.

When we brought Mark into our house for the first time at five days of age, his brother, Mike, two and one-half years old at the time, stood on a chair and looked into the bassinet and tried to pick him up and Charles told him, "NO! you can not pick him up."

Mike, looked at both of us with a frown on his brow and said, "Well take him back then."

****

When we were young parents, with two young boys, we turned down many invitations to attend parties because we did not want to take our two boys to the party and worry about them getting into something. We could count on Mark exploring the house.

Before we had children, we had observed young couples with little children at parties who completely ignored their children while the sweet little things pulled all the pots and pans out of the homeowner's pantry.

We did not want that reputation, so we declined many invitations.

****

Mark was different from his older brother, Mike, in several ways and it showed up early. At six months of age, Mike enjoyed being picked up and held by almost anyone, while Mark seemed to only want those he knew to hold him.

Mike could entertain himself as a young boy with toy soldiers, etc. Mark had to have interaction with others.

If Mike was in a corner of a room with his soldiers set up in mock battle and Mark entered the room, he would look around to see if anyone was watching, and if he thought the coast was clear, he would run through Mike's army and kick them in different directions.

Needless to say, this started a real war, which resulted in a truce only when Mama or Daddy entered the room.

****

Mike's niche was sports, while Mark's niche was entertaining people, whether they wanted to be entertained or not.

I recall one Easter on the way home from church, when Mark was two years old, he was mad at us about something and he was standing in the back seat, with the windows rolled down, and threw his hat out the window. (This was before we had air conditioning or seat belts in our car).

This was his way of making his point that he was independent. Guess who got a spanking when he got home?

****

In 1961 we took a family vacation and visited Charles' older brother, Gene, a Psychiatrist living in Los Angles.

Charles told him that he couldn't figure out our two boys, ages three and five.

He asked Charles what he meant and Charles said, "If I ask them what they want to eat, one will say shrimp and the other will say hamburger."

My brother-in-law told us something we have never forgotten. He said, "They are competing for your attention. When you are with both of them, you are not with either one of them."

After hearing that, Charles started spending more time with them one at a time and the friction between them seemed to diminish.

****

At an early age, Mark would make a funny face anytime he saw someone point a camera at him.

We threw a swimming party for Mark's third grade class and had all the children line up along the side of the pool and asked them how many could swim. Every one of the eight and nine year old students raised their hands.

I then had three of them at a time enter the shallow end of the pool and swim across the shallow end.

Over half of them could not swim. So we discovered that our son, Mark, was not the only child in history that could embellish.

****

Mark was very inquisitive as a young boy and was always checking things out. One time, when he was nine, I was driving in our subdivision and noticed Mark's bicycle along with two other bicycles in a ditch. I stopped the car and walked over to a bush on the other side of the ditch, having seen smoke rising up from behind the bush.

Guess who, along with two other nine-year-old boys was smoking a cigarette?

Needless to say, Mark experienced a lecture and a spanking administered by his Dad that night.

****

Mark kept us prayed up. We wanted to find his niche and finally found it when I took him to audition for a musical at the Houston Music Theatre.

Mark played in several musical plays in Houston, Texas and always received great reviews.

Mark won every audition he entered, even when he auditioned for the Bill Gaither Vocal Band.

When Mark was practicing for his musical plays, the tension around our house always seemed to lighten up.

Mike was always proud of his brother in these musicals. One time he advised a lady sitting next to him in the audience, "That boy in the play is my brother!"

I looked at the lady as she looked at Mike, and she smiled and said, "Really!"

Mike was smiling as though he had just won a great prize.

Mark being in various musicals in Houston, also brought him popularity in his class and school.

All of a sudden, he was a celebrity. His hyperactivity was being channeled in a new direction.

When Mike was thirteen and Mark was eleven, Charles bought both of them a motorized trail bike with the specific instructions that they could ride their bikes in the woods behind our house, but never on the street.

Guess who was caught by a Highway Patrolman riding his unlicensed motorbike on the public road?

This six-foot-six-inch Highway Patrolman showed up at our house with Mark in tow and announced to me that he was going to issue me a ticket because my son was on a public road riding an unlicensed motorbike.

I told the Highway Patrolman, "His Father purchased the motorbike, make the ticket out to him."

That night when Charles arrived home, I presented him the ticket.

Guess who had the privilege of explaining to the Judge how our eleven-year-old son happened to be on an unlicensed motorbike on a public road?

Fortunately, Charles knew the Judge, having practiced in his Court. The Judge thought it was not too serious and dismissed the ticket. So Charles won Mark's first traffic ticket.

Guess whose trail bike was sold the next day?

****

We discovered early that Mark is very tender hearted. On a vacation trip to Tennessee when Mark was eleven, we were driving on a one-way gravel mountain road, when a small animal, probably an opossum, ran under the car and the car struck the animal, and as we looked back we saw the animal flopping in the bushes.

Mark wanted us to stop and see if we could help the animal. Charles advised him we could not stop because we were on a narrow one-way mountain road and other cars were behind us.

Mark was very upset for several hours. He is still very tender hearted.

****

We did not have a Mark Lowry going around the country telling stories about hyperactivity. But we did have a great pediatrician who was very helpful with fatherly wisdom.

You may have heard Mark in some of his concerts tell about the time he carried a note to his sixth grade teacher after she intercepted one of his many notes he wrote in class and passed to various fellow classmates. She asked him why he did not write something other people could understand. He would make up words and put these words no one knew in his famous notes.

That particular evening we had some friends, Duke and Carlene Westover, over for supper (I am from Texas and it is Breakfast, Lunch and Supper).

During this particular evening the husband of the visiting couple, Duke Westover, gave Mark this saying: "Your feeble attempt to participate in any intelligent conversation only goes to show your pathetic lack of mental ability."

After supper, Mark addressed that saying to his teacher and signed it, "Sincerely, Mark Lowry."

The next day he handed it to his teacher and she marched him to the principal's office and he got a three-day vacation.

His Daddy had promised Mark before this event that if he were expelled for any of his activities, he would give him a spanking every day he was expelled.

When Charles arrived home that afternoon, I told him of the day's current events and that Mark was sitting in his room waiting for his spanking.

Charles grievously trudged up the stairs to his room and read the note from the teacher. Before Charles gave him his first of three daily spankings, he gave him some good legal advice and advised him that if he ever wrote anything like that again, "Don't sign it!"

****

Mark received his last spanking at the ripe old age of fifteen for talking back to me.

Charles told me that when he entered Mark's room to give him his spanking, he appeared more calm than he had ever seen him prior to a spanking. Charles asked him if he knew why he was getting this spanking, and he said, "Yes sir, I talked back to Mama."

Charles said he then told him to bend over the bed and proceeded to spank him with a belt. The first swat made a thud that sounded like hitting a hollow log.

Charles realized that Mark had added padding to the target area. He then advised him to undress and sure enough, Mark had put on several pair of underwear.

His Daddy had him remove the excess underwear and proceeded with the correction.

****

Watching two boys grow up was very rewarding. I remember when Mike was a senior in high school, they borrowed our car for their double date with two sisters. Two Saturday nights in a row they called at 11: 30 PM and informed their Daddy that the car ran out of gas.

The second Saturday night Charles carried gas to them, he informed both of them, "E" on the gas gauge stands for "Empty" not "Enough."

They thought if they could make it home, Daddy would fill up the car for their next week.

****

As young parents, we realized our responsibility was to raise our children in the nurture and admonition of the Lord, JESUS CHRIST.

We also realized that we loved our Dads and they administered many spankings to our target area and we as adults did not hate our Dads.

So with that understanding of life, we proceeded to raise our children in church, with love and according to biblical principals. I am sure we made many mistakes, but they were all made with the foremost thought that what we did was for the best interest of our children's future.

Today we are very proud of all three of our children and seven grandchildren. It is very rewarding to see our son, Mike, and daughter, Melissa, raising their children in the nurture and admonition of the LORD JESUS CHRIST. I know if Mark married and had children, he would do the same thing.

Ephesians 6:4 "And, ye fathers, provoke not your children to wrath: but bring them up in the nurture and admonition of the Lord."

The Book of Proverbs has been a great source of strength in raising our children and especially our Hyperactive son, Mark.

These are some of the main verses we relied on for our wisdom:

Proverbs 1:8   My son, hear the instruction of thy father, and forsake not the law of thy mother.

Proverbs 3:12 For whom the Lord loveth he correcteth; even as a father the son in whom he delighteth.

Proverbs 4:1   Hear, ye children, the instruction of a father, and attend to know understanding.

Proverbs 6:20 My son, keep thy father's commandment, and forsake not the law of thy mother.

Proverbs 13:1 A wise son heareth his father's instruction; but a scorner heareth not rebuke.

<u>Proverbs 13:24</u>   He that spareth his rod hateth his son: but he that loveth him chasteneth him betimes.

<u>Proverbs 22:6</u> Train up a child in the way he should go; and when he is old, he will not depart from it.

<u>Proverbs 22:15</u>   Foolishness is bound in the heart of a child; but the rod of correction shall drive it far from him.

To all you young parents and future parents, if you will take to heart the above scriptures and apply this wisdom in raising your children, whether they are hyperactive or not, IT WORKS!!!

As I said earlier, I taught Child Psychology at Liberty University for over seventeen years and speak at many Women's Conferences each year. I have asked my students and the ladies at the conference each year, "How many of you were spanked as a young child?" Most hands go up. Then I ask, "How many of you are still mad about it?" All the hands go down. Godly discipline is still God's way.

During Charles' forty-five years of law practice he has told many of his clients who were anxious over their legal problems the story about Grandfather Clock going to a psychiatrist. As Grandfather Clock enters the psychiatrist's office he is very nervous. The psychiatrist asks Grandfather Clock why he is so upset. Grandfather Clock responds with, "Do you realize how many ticks I have to tick a year?" The psychiatrist asks, "Well, how many ticks do you have to tick at a time?" Grandfather Clock answers, "One." The psychiatrist tells Grandfather Clock, "Well, take life one tick at a time!"

Remember, never take advice from an Old Maid psychologist on how to raise your children! And, if you go to a counselor, be sure they are a Christian Counselor.

Someday you too may have the opportunity to look back on how you raised your children, and hopefully you will be able to say you followed biblical principles, even though it was not politically correct.

Mark, makes this statement in many of his concerts, "If you have a hyperactive child be careful how you treat that child, you may end up on a Comedy Video someday".

The stories Mark has told around the country about his childhood were not funny when we lived them. But, they are funny today and we enjoy every one.

Article on "Mouth In Motion" video

Here are some reporters' comments from various interviews:

Mark said, "I never tried to be funny. All I did was talk while the little old man handling the tape player, turned over the tape for my next song. During that time I would tell the audience about something that happened to me during my childhood and they would start laughing. I thought they were laughing at me, but they were laughing at my stories, not my testimony."

Mark Lowry is a south Texas boy who grew up going to church and minding his Mama and Daddy, most of the time. Mark was a hyperactive child who had what is now known as ADHD (Attention Deficit Hyperactivity Disorder).

Mark says, "I had it before people knew what it was. Back then in the 1960's they called it B.R.A.T. I got a whipping every day; sometimes two or three times a day. I thought it was normal; you brush your teeth, get a whipping, go to bed.

All I knew was that there weren't enough trees to make enough paper for all the notes my teacher would have to send home with me."

Mark finds humor in the Christian life, always touching the heart as he touches the funny bone, and with his Word album "Mouth In Motion," he stretches out to find a funny side to the music of his fellow Christian recording artists.

"This video includes plenty of Mark's stand-up comedy, but his stories lead into parodies of Christian hits, exploring such comedy-rich areas as blind dates, plastic surgery and singing with Sandi Patty."

Mark has a disdain for flying. He said, "I used to sit in the back of planes 'cause I'd never seen a plane back into a mountain."

In "Mouth In Motion" he is assigned a seat on an exit row which requires him to help passengers off in the case of a crash. He says, "I'll help 'em off the plane, if they can follow my wide rear-end through that door."

Then he sings a song written by Martha Bolton and Phil Maderia titled "First Class, Wrong Flight."

Mark does a parody of Amy Grant's "Every Heartbeat" with a song titled, "Every Teacher." He uses this song to tell about his problem childhood in school. He says, "Several of my teachers are still in therapy."

Mark also says, "He brought prayer back to school, because all his teachers prayed he would pass."

In this video Mark plays his teacher, proving turnabout is fair play.

As a member of the Christian music community, Mark dreamed of the day he could sing with Sandi

Patty. In his prior video, "The Last Word" Sandi played a fan asking for an autograph and Mark snubbed her saying, "Some other time, some other place," a song Sandi sung with Wayne Watson. Now in this video Sandi gets her revenge when Mark is begging her to sing with him, she responds, "Where all my friends won't see and no one knows me and I'll hide my face."

Then after watching an open heart surgery, Mark says, "Jesus doesn't want to get into your left ventricle and watch blood go by, He wants into your life."

In this video we hear Mark say, "My favorite verse is, "And it came to pass…" He interprets it, "Whatever we're going through, it didn't come to stay." Then he says, "You young 18-year-old jocks that have muscles in your earlobes, enjoy them. They will pass."

Next Mark sings a song of faith and self-confidence. With lyrics by Mark and music by Phil Maderia, "I don't have to stay where I am today, because this too shall pass.

This video, "Mouth In Motion" takes the audience through a host of emotions and leaves them feeling better for the journey.

Mark Lowry was born in Houston, Texas in 1958. His mother Beverly, a psychology professor, played piano in church; his father Charles, a lawyer, was a church deacon. Mark obtained from his parents the combination of music and humor that make him what he is today.

Mark says, "Dad is very unmusical. He's funny, but very quiet—he doesn't care if anybody hears his wit or not. Mother can sing. She's loud, but not funny —I picked that up from her. I inherited my humor from my Father and my decibels from Mom."

Mark played in several musical productions in Houston at the age of nine and ten such as "The Music Man" with Hal March and Susan Watson and "Annie Get Your Gun" with Kay Star. At the age of 11 he sang at the International Song Festival in Nashville, Tennessee and after singing one song, he landed a recording contract and also a booking contract with a talent agency. He went on to record two albums, including one backed by the London Symphony Orchestra.

At fourteen, Mark's voice began to change and he resumed a normal school life by going off correspondence and attending regular high school. After graduation, he enrolled in Liberty Baptist College, (now Liberty University) in Lynchburg, Virginia.

In 1976 he changed his major from business to music and started traveling with an evangelistic team. This team consisted of Charles Hughes, the Preacher, David Musselman, the Piano player, Richard Bernier, the driver of their van and Mark as the singer.

On March 17, 1978 around 1 AM, their van skidded on a patch of ice, bounced off the guardrail on the right side of I-81 about 2 miles south of I-81 exit 12 near Carlisle, Pennsylvania and then skidded back across the middle of the highway and met a Mack tractor-trailer which struck their van in the left side.

Richard Bernier suffered bruised and broken ribs and black eyes. David Musselman sustained bruised and broken ribs, Charles Hughes suffered severe head injuries and was in a coma for ten weeks. Mark was thrown out of the van, sustaining one broken leg, two broken ankles, broken collar bone and several broken ribs, totaling eleven broken bones. He subsequently developed Fat Embolism and the orthopedic surgeon told his mother that he would either die or be mentally retarded.

Mark, in many of his concerts since then has made the statement, "Well, I did not die."

After many of his concerts, parents and grandparents tell him that his stories about his childhood gives them hope for the hyperactive child in their family.

Mark Lowry has been delivering hilarious, G-rated comedy to sell-out crowds for years on the road, in his popular recordings, and on his award-winning videos. His "Mouth In Motion" video was recently certified gold, and his video project "Remotely Controlled" went gold almost immediately — another indication of his remarkable success.

He hit the bookshelves in 1996 with his quasi-autobiography "Out Of Control" and has released two books of a new series of children books all about his own created character — "Piper the Hyper Mouse."

Mark says, "My stories are so wrapped up in church that God gets in there anyway. People don't mind you giving them the Gospel as long as you do it naturally. The Gospel is throughout all of my experiences. The Message can't help but come out."

NOTE: Some of the above comments were from Mama and some of the above comments were taken from CMO Artists at the following website:

http://www.cmo.com/cmo/cmo/data/mlowry.htm
and,
Artist Direction agency at the following website:
http://www.artistdirectionagency.com/
biomarklowry.htm

Mark's Testimony
June 5, 2006
So far...

Thirty-three years ago today, I asked Jesus to come into my heart. It doesn't seem that long ago. I can still remember it. I knelt under a tree and prayed. Our denomination calls it 'getting saved'.

After that, I wanted to tell everybody about Jesus.

I remember getting on an airplane and being afraid that if I didn't tell the person sitting next to me about Jesus, they would go to Hell and their blood would be on my hands. So, I kept trying to figure out a way to ask, "If you were to die today, would you go to Heaven? I finally asked. It felt awkward. She was a nun.

Fast forward Thirty-three years.

This past Memorial Day, I had a cookout at my house. I ended up talking to a few people on the back porch (which is my favorite spot). Somehow, the conversation got around to God. I don't know how that always happens. Guess it's because there's nothing more interesting. It's the never-ending discussion.

If I recall correctly, these new friends consisted of a former Mormon missionary, a United Pentecostal, a

Catholic or two, various and sundry other creeds... and George.

George was raised in a home that was 'agnostic'. At his house, religion didn't figure in. "But," he said, "I believe there is something after this life."

That caught my ear.

"Why do you believe that?" I asked.

He sputtered to a stop. He had continued onto another part of his story and didn't know what I was talking about. "Believe what?" he asked.

"You said you believe there is something after this life. Why do you believe that?"

He said he didn't know.

Everybody started talking and telling what they believed and why.

Why do we believe there's something beyond this life?

What causes us to even consider it?

How could we long for something we've never known?

I crave Blue Bell ice cream. Sometimes, I even 'long' for it. You see, I've tasted Blue Bell ice cream. I know what Blue Bell ice cream tastes like. I'm going to have some right now....

I'm back.

Why do I believe there's something beyond this life?

God.

My DNA remembers God.

He made a very good first impression.

I believe our DNA echoes with the memory of His goodness. His breath is still in us (Genesis 2:7). We are His broken image (Genesis 1:27).

I have a dog. To my knowledge, he doesn't remember God. And he longs for nothing but to be scratched and thrown a treat. There isn't anything in him that thinks there is something after this life.

At least, he's never spoken to me about it.

When it was my turn to tell why I believe there's something after this life, I told my friends that I came from God, got lost and Jesus has come to take me home.

But, a funny thing happened. As I was beginning to tell my story, I felt a lump rising in my throat and tears starting to burn in my eyes.

(Oh my gosh, I feel like I'm on a Gaither video... where's the camera?)

My voice was shaky. "It's because of Jesus," I said. "He started it. He loved me first. And He proved it by dying for my sins and rising from the dead. I believe that more than I believe I'm sitting here."

"We all come from the same God. We may not agree about where the 'longing' comes from but there's no denying it. Well, I am beginning to find that my 'longing' is satisfied by the love of Jesus. Getting to know Him is like finding breadcrumbs along the path giving you a little taste of what's waiting at the house."

"What I'm trying to say is, Jesus won my heart."

—Mark Lowry

Chapter Ten
Establishing a Godly Home Environment

It is very important that we have a Godly home environment, especially with hyperactive children. I want to insert in this book sections taken from my book, "How to Establish a Godly Home Environment."

I taught psychology at Liberty University for seventeen years and started to college when I was 46. Before starting, I was scared my brain would not work. I asked my husband who encouraged me to go to college, "Do you know how old I will be in four years when I finish?"

His answer, "How old will you be in four years if you don't go?"

My daughter, Missy, was in the eighth grade. She said, "Please finish before I get to college." My son, Mark, was a senior at Liberty. He pleaded with me, "Don't start to college until I get out. I don't want to pass you in the halls, and I sure don't want to sit beside you in class." So when he graduated in May, I enrolled for the fall semester.

My daughter, Missy, as a freshman, was in the first psychology class I taught at Liberty University after receiving my Masters Degree from Lynchburg College.

I was blessed to take my first psychology course from a great man of God, Dr. Philip Captain. He put Christ in every lesson. I was hooked, and changed my major from education to psychology.

Personally, I do not feel that psychology is a science because there is very little that can be empirically proven. Most psychological research comes from very subjective experiences. We know that certain childhood experiences can cause us to have certain feelings.

Though psychology can tell us why we have certain emotions, it cannot tell us one thing to do about it. The answer to all of those problems is in one Person, the Lord Jesus Christ.

Second Corinthians 5:17 says, "If any man be in Christ, he is a new creature. Old things are passed away, behold, all things are become new." When our son, Mark, at the age of fourteen, made Jesus the Lord of his life, we saw a drastic change in his life. The summer he accepted Jesus as Lord of his life, he read the whole bible from Genesis through Revelation, including the maps.

As a new creature in Christ, we can't change our experiences, but we can change our reactions to those experiences. God's Word says that when we accept Christ we have a supernatural power to forgive and to overcome the "old things" in our lives. In fact, He says that they are passed away and "all things are new."

The Holy Spirit of God who lives within us gives us the power to overcome.

That same Holy Spirit gives you the ability to be a godly person and establish a godly home environment.

Did God have an ideal for the human family? When God created Adam and Eve, what did He intend for the home environment to be? Do we have His ideal homes today? If not, how far are we from His ideal?

In the Garden of Eden, God created Adam and Eve to fellowship with Him. He wanted to be with them in the cool of the day. In love, God warned them not to eat of the tree of knowledge of good and evil. He said if they did they would die.

Then satan entered the scene and told Eve a half-truth. He told her that she would not die if she tasted the fruit of the tree. He meant that she would not die physically, while God had meant that she would die spiritually. Well, we know the story. Eve believed satan instead of God and used her influence to convince Adam to eat of the tree also.

Scripture says that Eve was deceived. Adam was not deceived; he knew that he was disobeying God. Nevertheless, sin entered the world by way of a deceived woman, and fellowship with God was broken.

God's ideal plan for the family is for the husband and wife to worship and honor Him in their relationship with Him, with each other and with their family. Ever since that first step of disobedience to God, mankind has struggled with sin. However, there is a way to overcome sin's stranglehold in our homes.

First and foremost, to have a godly home environment we must be committed to God and to the Lordship of Jesus Christ. We must want to obey God and do His will. Christ must be the head of the home. He must be the center of our lives. He will not share His glory with another.

Deuteronomy 6:5 says, "And thou shalt love the Lord thy God with all thine heart and with all thy soul, and with all thy might." When we really love something or someone we will die for that thing or person. We must love God more than anything or anyone.

When your hyperactive child sees your commitment to Christ, that child will want to know more about Jesus.

We must fear God in reverence. Deuteronomy 10: 12 says, "What doth the Lord thy God require of thee, but to fear the Lord thy God, to walk in all His ways, and to love Him, and to serve the Lord thy God with all thy heart and with all thy soul."

Fearing the Lord is healthy. Like a child fears His parents, we should fear God. This fear represents a special respect and trust and acknowledgement of higher authority. It's a scary thing to see the lack of fear toward God that Christians have today.

I was fortunate and blessed to have a loving earthly Father who also taught me to obey him. I had a healthy fear of my Dad and it kept me out of trouble.

The fear of God will keep us walking in His ways. Our ways are not His ways sometimes, but His ways are always best. Walking in His ways will keep us out of trouble and will present a good example to others. We are to know God and apply His words to our lives. The book of Proverbs will definitely assist you in raising all of your children and especially the hyperactive child.

First: To establish a godly home environment, that is pleasing to God, parents must begin with uniting together as husband and wife in willful obedience to a loving God.

Second: For husband and wife to have a godly home environment, they must commit to each other in a stable and fulfilling marriage. It is very important that both be committed to Christ first, before marriage. We are not to be unequally yoked with unbelievers.

My Mom used to tell me, "Every date is a possible mate." She very carefully watched who I dated, and I am thankful she did. She knew more about life than I did at that time. She was my protector. I was not allowed to date a non-Christian, nor was I allowed to date a non-Baptist. Yes, I said "allowed." My parents controlled my choice of dates. That might seem harsh by today's standards, but psychology tells you that the more 'alike' you are, the easier your marriage will be and the better decisions you will make, that means spiritually, socially, economically and in every other way. Marriage is hard in and of itself, but the more 'different' we are to start with, the harder it will be ultimately. I am thankful that my mother guided me.

The biblical roles of men and women are different. Men are masculine. They are to be the husbands, Fathers, and spiritual leaders of the home. Women are feminine. Femininity means one thing --- beauty. Spiritual beauty is available to all. Women are to be wives, Mothers, educators, and encouragers. Psalm 144:12 calls us "the cornerstones."

The Mother role of women is spiritually cursed. We become emotionally tied to the lives of our children. As the child hurts, we hurt. We cannot prevent our children from hurting. We have to teach them how to cope with pain, but we can never prevent it. We will hurt when they hurt. "When women become Mothers, they wear their hearts outside their own bodies forever." But, we will rejoice when our children rejoice.

Many times as a young Mother I felt like I failed when my children would do something wrong. This is especially true when raising a hyperactive child.

One thing my husband and I agreed on and that was we would never argue in front of our children, and to this day we have kept that promise. I am not saying we never argued, but not in front of our children. Therefore our children never had to worry about Mom and Dad divorcing.

A Mom and Dad in agreement on a child's behavior, leaves no room for the child to play the two of you against each other.

Our children will never be perfect, but we can and must give them our unconditional love. Their home should be a place where they can make mistakes and know that their parents will be there for them.

Helping our children have good self-esteem should be a top priority. We can do that by being an encourager to them and not expecting perfection.

By the time a child is 10 years old, he or she has a success or failure identity. Believing that you are a failure will help you be a failure. We all believe that because we think something, it is correct. You can literally make things happen so that you won't have to change the way you think.

Believing that you are a success will help you be a success. We need to help our children feel good about themselves and believe that they are successful. Certainly, they are successful in our eyes.

The nurture starts very early in life. I'm reminded of Mamie McCullough's story about the time her children were making mud pies with the neighborhood children. The children asked her to come outside and judge the mud pies. She went back in the house and cut ribbons for the judging. She cut three blue ribbons and all the rest were red and white ribbons. She went back outside and put the three first place blue ribbons on her three children's pies. All of the rest of the children received second and third place ribbons. One little neighborhood boy said, "That's not fair. You gave all of your kids first place and the rest of us got second and third place." Mamie said she looked him in the eye and said, "If you want a first place ribbon, you go get your mother to come judge the pies."

Mamie said, "If your children can't be winners at home, where will they be winners?" She also said that someday she is sure that she and her children will sit around the Thanksgiving Day table and laugh about the time she gave them first place over the other kids in the neighborhood.

We have to practice being positive parents. We need to establish a positive emotional climate in the home and avoid being critical. That is hard. We must rebuke satan. He tries to put us down as women. We tell ourselves we're not pretty enough, thin enough, or smart enough. He places those thoughts in our minds, and he is a liar. We must tell him so. If he can defeat us in our minds, we will never be what God has given us the potential to be as mothers.

Being a good Mother is a choice. That choice brings responsibilities that we cannot escape before God. Motherhood begins at conception, not birth.

The challenge that I give to you is to make a commitment of a minimum of six years per child to stay at home with that child as a full-time Mother. It would be wonderful if all Mothers could take that challenge.

Research shows that the most critical time in producing healthy children is during the first six years of life. The most impact comes from the influence of the Mother. We establish in our children a sense of security or insecurity, and we help them attach to us.

The first year of life is probably the most important. Studies show that the majority of women do stay home. And recently many are returning home. Some will say that they have to work. I agree. Some do have to work. I feel that it would be wrong for any of us to tell anyone else that they are not doing what God wants them to do simply because they work outside the home.

The number one reason that women work is "divorce." Second is single Mothering. If we could save the marriages, we could decrease the number of women working outside the home.

If you are 25 and have three children, 2 years apart and you commit 6 years to each child to stay home that will amount to 10 years. This still leaves 30 years for a career.

As you are raising your children, you can continue your education. Liberty University has a program called DLP. It means Distance Learning Program. You can go to class on video and it's accredited. Go to school while the kids take naps. Or go to a local college one-day a week.

Many women who were full-time mothers now have a career. I am one such woman. I stayed home with my children. I taught piano. Today, that would be considered a "home industry." A home industry means you work from your home and get paid. With the advent of the computer, women can have many home industries. We may have to be creative but there are many things we can do to help the family income without leaving the home at all.

If at all possible, make that commitment to be a full-time Mom. Fathers should make a commitment, also, to spend extra time with their families.

I am so glad that Charles took time to tell our children bedtime stories. Our children still remember those stories very well. He used to record them as he told them on an old reel to reel tape recorder and then get his secretary to type them from the tape. He recently found some that he had put in a file. He is in the process of publishing them for parents to read to their children.

Instead of trying to reach a peak at the age of thirty, Fathers need to try for forty, when the children will be past the six-year commitment. In old age none of us will sit in a nursing home and say, "I wish I'd spent more time at the office."

To those of you who are young marrieds or never married; commit yourself to staying out of debt during the first five to ten years of marriage. Young people want to immediately have everything their parents have without working up to it. That is fantasy. It will take two and a half incomes to pay for all of that kind of debt.

Let me give you Dr. Philip Captain's rules for staying out of debt:

Start with faith in God instead of faith in your job. "My God shall supply all of your needs."

1. Live only on a husband's income. Do not budget your standard of living based on two incomes.

2. Use the wife's income to make major purchases such as washers, dryers, and more. Save the wife's income in the bank in a separate account. Watch for bargains and only pay cash.

3. The car is a depreciating asset. It is for a function, not an extension of one's self-esteem.

4. We as parents must decide between things or children. Children care most about time with their parents, not about big houses and big cars.

So how are we going to establish and maintain a "Godly Home Environment?" By living under God's blueprint of what constitutes a family.

We as parents must live as godly examples of a family and have a godly home environment for our children to grow up and duplicate that in their families. Every generation is getting farther and farther away from God's plan.

A godly home environment must begin before marriage. Our young people must choose a mate who is as committed to the Lordship of Christ as they are.

And we who are already married must draw a line in the sand and say, for me and my house we will live as close as we can to God's blueprint of a godly home environment. We can't have a perfect godly home environment because of our sin nature and the sin nature of our spouse and children.

Some people come from homes where their sin nature was never dealt with by their parents. So we have to start where we are. I believe that God will hold us individually responsible for how we deal with His blueprint for a godly home environment. I say "individually" because some know more about God's principles than others.

Those of us who do know what God intended for a family must tell others. We must get the family back on the right track. We must not listen to satan's lies anymore. I believe that all families want to survive.

Many families are a wreck because they believed satan's lies. Are those families hopeless? No. They can survive.

Martin DeHaan II calls surviving families those who start with the situation as it is, and takes practical, biblical steps to ensure that the family is characterized by:

Proper roles;

A high degree of unity;

A desire for spiritual growth;

Actions that are dictated by love;

Forgiveness and understanding.

If these traits are found in a home, the family will do more than hang together – it will thrive.

This is not to suggest that there won't be problems. Surviving families, DeHaan says, aren't composed of Precious Moments figurines that stare blankly past life's struggles. Families that survive aren't exempt from rebellious teens, mischievous little boys, occasionally selfish Fathers, and sometimes over-bearing Mothers. But surviving families are marked by a commitment to one another, a love for the Lord, and a strong desire to make the family a good place to be, despite faults and imperfection. Does that sound like your family? It can. Any Christian family – once its members are maintaining a right relationship to God – can thrive in today's world.

With dedication to God's principles for family living, your family can be safe at home and can be very close to God's blueprint for a godly home environment.

What a wonderful Mother Mary must have been to Jesus. But she was not perfect, because she had a sin nature as we all do. We can't be perfect Mothers either. But we can choose to be good Mothers and Fathers can choose to be good Fathers.

First of all, we need to know Jesus as our Savior. If you don't know Him today, I urge you to accept His sacrifice for your sins, or one day you will pay the price yourself by spending eternity in a Lake of Fire. Sin demands atonement. Jesus paid the price for that. What a wonderful Savior He is. He can take your sins and make you white as snow. Under the Lordship of Christ, you will be able to be the Mother or Father that he wants you to be to that hyperactive child as well as Mother or Father to your other children that are not hyperactive. He wants you to follow Him and His leading in your life as you raise your children. Or under His Lordship you can be the young unmarried woman or unmarried man that He wants you to be. The bottom line is that we will be women and men who have overcome the curse through the Lordship of Christ. And we can be what God wants us to be. As we seek His leading in our lives. He will reveal His will for us.

Chapter Eleven
Remarks
(Conclusions)

In the Introduction of this book, I stated that I would tell how we raised a "Hyperactive" child. I also stated that we are not perfect parents, nor have there ever been any perfect parents. We did not raise a perfect "Hyperactive" son. I have quoted some noted psychologists in this book pertaining to raising children.

My concerns in writing this book was whether or not I could really help Mothers and Fathers who are raising a "Hyperactive" child. I pray so.

If I could live my life over, there are many things I would do differently such as trying to see things through the eyes of our "Hyperactive" son, realizing that a child thinks as a child and not an adult. Also, I would not be under the assumption that my child's actions are extensions of my arms. I would be more concerned about pleasing God than neighbors, relatives, or anybody else while raising our "Hyperactive" son. I definitely would hold him back from starting school, until he was one year older, due to the fact that he turned six only two months before he started to first grade. This would have given him an additional year to reach the maturity level of most of the other children in his class, and he would not be one of the youngest in his class. I really believe this would have made a BIG difference in his behavior in school.

Mark has a website, "www.MarkLowry.com" with a link to my website, "www.BevLowry.com. For many years, he told the audiences at his concerts, and on his videos that he was a "Hyperactive" child. He also said, "When I was young, the term was not 'ADHD,' it was 'Brat.'" He also informed people at those concerts, "My Mother teaches Child Psychology at Liberty University." This generated many-many emails asking me how I raised Mark. Mark also forwarded many emails to me from people asking questions about "Hyperactivity" behavior. I tried to answer all of those emails.

In the emails I received from parents, they expressed their fears and concerns they were having in raising their "Hyperactive" child. At almost every one of my speaking engagements, I have Mothers, Grandmothers, Aunts and Relatives of "Hyperactive" children tell me that they have a "Mark Lowry." Then they proceed to ask me how we raised Mark.

My husband, Charles, played a very important role in Mark's upbringing, especially in the matter of discipline.

When the boys were in elementary school, each night at nine, after they had taken their bath, Charles would enter their bedroom and tell them an adventure story in which they were the heroes. He always put two boys in the story, named Mike and Mark. After the story, we would pray with them and tell them we loved them and hug and kiss them goodnight.

As stated in this book, we prayed to God for wisdom and tried to find Mark's "niche."

I thank the Lord that I was observant and "Fearless" when talking to Mark's teachers and principal of his elementary school. I am especially referring to the time I saw Mark with his head on his desk, asleep, in the first part of third grade, after taking Ritalin. I learned that the teacher had placed him behind a partition in her classroom for three weeks prior to the time I saw him asleep in class. That gave me the God given "Fearlessness" and urgency to move Mark out of that class and take him off Ritalin.

So, I say to you parents, be very observant, and "Fearless" in your actions in raising your "Hyperactive" child. God has loaned that child to you and you are accountable to God for the way you raise your child.

When I say fearless, I don't mean attacking a teacher. She has her hands full. I never talked ugly to Mark about a teacher. I worked behind the scenes to try and help him. He had to be there and have respect for the teacher. If I had talked ugly about her to him, he could not have respected her.

Believe me, that child will grow up very quickly with the probability of becoming your best friend and an adult of whom you will be very proud.

One thing I want to point out to every parent, is to reach out to your "Hyperactive" child and try to look at the various situations through his or her eyes.

Also, look up the definitions of "Hyperactivity" and "Creativity." You will find the same characteristics.

The "Hyperactive" child that God gave us, is the adult that for many years has been a blessing to many, many people. He has given parents hope for their "Hyperactive" child. As I said earlier, this "Hyperactive" child is the adult who wrote the song, "Mary Did You Know?"

As a side note to "Mary Did You Know?" Mark can not read or write music. He wrote the words to "Mary Did You Know?" and during five years after writing the song, he asked several professionals to write the music to the song. He never liked their proposed music. He had one professional tell him he had "Mary Did You Know?" too many times in the song. To which he replied, "I am not going to take any of them out of the song."

Then one day on Bill Gaither's bus, he handed the written words to Buddy Green, and asked him to put music to the song. A few days later, Buddy called Mark and sang the song with his music and "Mary Did

You Know?" was completed. That was five years of patience. Not bad for a "Hyperactive" person.

I am placing some testimonies in the APPENDIX. These were received from grateful parents and various individuals expressing their THANKS to me for raising a son who loves "JESUS" and being the kind of person that has a love for people. A person who actually cares for the ones he encounters along his life's path.

I conclude with some references in the APPENDIX for you to do your own research on the subject of "Hyperactivity" / ADD and ADHD.

"Yes" is the answer I give to many, many people who say, "I bet you are really proud of Mark." Charles and I are very thankful for the way God has blessed Mark with the ability to communicate with people. He makes them laugh and gives them serious thoughts about "JESUS." He gives the plan of salvation in a simple language, even a small child can understand.

He is a very tender hearted, warm, caring and loving son to his Mother and Dad as well as to his brother, Mike, sister, Melissa, their spouses and children.

He is very dedicated on his mission of taking the word of GOD to all that will see and hear him in person, on his website, in concerts and on videos. For he is not ashamed of the GOSPEL!

Over the past several years, at many of my speaking engagements, I jokingly told people that someday I was going to write a book about raising a "Hyperactive" son. Almost every time the people who heard this said, "Please do it soon!"

Finally, let me say, writing this book has been a way of reliving our struggles, and victories not only with raising our son, Mark, but in overcoming a lot of heartaches and pain we encountered from people who thought they had all the answers for a "Hyperactive" child. Only GOD has the answers, for He wrote the book—the "HOLY BIBLE." Ask for wisdom.

I want to give Mark credit for the title to this book. On more than one occasion, while attending one of his concerts, we heard him say, "My parents are going to write a book titled, 'How We Raised A Hyperactive Child And Lived To Tell About It." I added, "And You Can Too!"

May GOD Bless YOU and YOUR family in your journey through this life! My prayer is that if I don't meet you here on earth, I'll meet you on the street of gold in Heaven. The only way that is possible is that you either had or will have a saving experience of accepting JESUS as your Lord and Savior, for I accepted Him as my Savior at the age of eight. He is so faithful.

All you have to do, is with a repentant heart, confess to GOD that you are a sinner, for we are all sinners. Believe and acknowledge with all your heart that JESUS is the Son of GOD. That He was born of a virgin, lived a sinless life, died on the cross for your sins, was buried, rose the third day and now sits at the right hand of GOD the Father making intercession for you and all others that have accepted Him as Lord and Savior. For you see, He is GOD!

May GOD BLESS YOU as you raise or help raise that "Hyperactive" child. I am happy to admit, yes, I am thankful for Mark, as well as our other son, Mike, and his wife, Natashia, and their children, Chris, Courtney, Chad and Chelsea, and our daughter, Melissa, and her husband, Charlie, and their children, Zac and Katelyn.

Also, with all my heart and soul I am happy and thankful to admit that I am not ashamed of the GOSPEL!

—Bev Lowry

APPENDICES

(A) Testimonials of THANKS

(B) "Hyperactivity" ADD
    and ADHD References
    Ritalin Resources (and its dangers)

It has been reported that between the years of 1990-2000, over 569 children were hospitalized, 38 of them were life-threatening hospitalizations, and 186 died. For more information, go to www.RitalinDeath.com

Testimonials of Thanks

Some of the Testimonial Emails I and my daughter, Melissa, have received from people who have children diagnosed with ADD or ADHD, or with comments concerning Mark.

(1) Dear Beverly,
Our daughter, Dena, decided I'd been old-fashioned long enough and got me a new address and hooked me up!

How's that book coming? I've got to write to Mark and tell him he's been lots of places but I have one place he probably never thought he'd be...on our 50th Anniversary quilt, using the pictures you sent Dena.

Thanks...what memories!

The "older than God" teacher 3rd grade!
Ramona Hollan
13-Jun-2003 13:47:23

++++++++++++++

(2) Hello Mrs.Lowry, I just want to thank you for putting up with Mark all those years (and still doing so, I'm sure). And for raising him to love the Lord so much. Ya know, there aren't many people who would give the plan of Salvation at their

concerts because they would be afraid of hurting their image. I am so glad Mark is not afraid of that and I believe God has blessed him because of it. I missed your anniversary but I hope it was a happy one and I hope ya'll have many more to come.

My Pastor's wife has heard you speak and she says you are awesome. I hope, someday, to be able to hear you speak as well. Keep serving the Lord and tell Mark he should have you sing with him more often. You have a wonderful voice!

Deanna
27-Aug-2003 18:03:20

+++++++++++++++

(3) Cool website! I think yours is a real success story-if Mark was as bad as he says he is, and turned out so great, you are one awesome parent!
Angel
05-Sep-2003 20:04:27

+++++++++++++++

(4) I just went and seen Mark in Lakeland, Fl and he was so awesome in concert. I told him I have all his video's and that I just watched the one with you in it on Broadway and love the song you preformed. Your family has the gift of laughter and songs in your Heart God has Blessed you'll. He does so good sharing the

Love of God and he has made me look at life in a new light.

Thank you Mom Lowry.
Ed
 08-Sep-2003 23:37:44

++++++++++++++

(5) Dear Bev,
My husband is a Minister. We have 2 grown daughters. We now have an adopted son who is 9 years old. He was recently diagnosed with ADHD. He is a big Mark Lowry fan. He goes to sleep at night listening to one of Mark's CDs. He knows he can be anything he wants to be, even with ADHD, because Mark has. We appreciate so much Mark sharing his ADD with us.

It gives hope to children with learning problems. These special kids need that. I admire the wonderful job you and your husband did with your "special kid." Mark is a God gifted young man. Our prayers are with all of your family as you serve our Lord. Thank you and Mark for sharing a difficult part of your life. It is a great help to know this is a "doable" task of raising special boys.
Love in Christ, Sherry
27-Sep-2003 21:14:49

++++++++++++++
(6) I've wanted to say Thank You for a very long time.

My 2 oldest sons (7 & 8 yrs) have ADHD (So far my 2 yr old is the "perfect brother") and they absolutely adore Mark! They watch & scrutinize everything he does & says & I can see pieces of him in them because of that. And pieces of our Lord & Savior. Praise God for the light that shines thru him & you & your family. He has truly blessed our family & thru him you have as well. We are hoping to get to meet him when he comes to our city next month & someday I would love to meet you & thank you in person for the inspiration you are to myself & other mothers of ADHD kids. (And please, if you have any advice on how to deal w/them I'd love it!)

Thank you again & God Bless & Keep you.

Donna

26-Oct-2003 21:31:51

+++++++++++++++

(7) I just wanted to thank you for never giving up on your son, Mark. I know you have heard from thousands, yeah millions of fans how your son has touched so many lives. I have enjoyed his singing for decades and most recently his comedy for years.

Last October, my first born son was diagnosed ADHD. To say I was devastated was an understatement. I did like most, what did I do wrong? Did I do something wrong in the pregnancy? Did I let him watch too much TV as a toddler? Did I not discipline properly (the belief of most Baptists, I fear)?

But just a few weeks ago, I came across a VERY OLD tape of Mark's, probably done back in the late '70s, early '80s (I can't find it anywhere, except my copy from my old youth director). I remember Mark saying how he was a hyperactive child. I just finished watching "The Last Word" with James (our ADHD son) and he looked at me and said, "Mommie, his mommie got God to use him, too!" I just cried. I saw Mark perform this concert just after graduating from college in the early '90s, and didn't even realized I had "picked-up" your good night of "One day, God's gonna use you." James has heard that every night since his birth.

Thank you for all you and your husband did to raise a son to serve The LORD and be an example for sons like mine.

Now, when are you going to write that CHRISTIAN PARENTING book for us moms of ADHD boys??!!?!?! We sure could use it!!!
Melissa

++++++++++++++

(8) Mrs. Lowry,
I have been a fan of Mark's for several years now and feel like I know you from what I have heard him tell. I took the time to listen to some of his ADHD radio programs this morning (We do normally go to Church but we have that terrible stomach virus that is going around so I ended up staying at home so I decided to

visit Mark's website to listen to some of his work. I loved the tribute he did to Anthony Burger.) and was blessed by hearing the two of you sing together. I can't tell you the name of the song at the moment but it ministered to me. Thank you for loving Mark enough to bring him up loving the Lord. He has blessed me and my family for many years. I was saddened to hear of his diagnosis of MS but believe that God is going to use this time in Mark's life for His glory! My brother in law also has MS and was diagnosed back in 1998. He has good days and bad days but most of the bad days are when he is struggling with the steroid injections that he has to take frequently. He is still able to go hunting every weekend and they were just blessed with the birth of a son. They worried about having children hearing that MS could be passed down to the baby but they believe that God will keep the baby from that disease. He stays quite active though so we are praying for his complete healing.

I feel that you are a true woman of faith and when I heard that you had your own website I just had to visit. I have seen the pictures of Missy's daughter Katelyn on Marks website and had to share that my daughters name (though spelled differently) is also Kaitlyn. Thank you again for sharing your love for the Lord with your son because he is a blessing to thousands of people. Sincerely,
Sherri

+++++++++++++

(9) This is neat to hear about, huh?!
Subj: Your Brother and My Brother
Date: Thursday, December 9, 2004 3:08:52 AM
To: Melissa, Mark's Sister

Dear Missy,

Sitting here tonight, I have tears of joy in my eyes . I hope you don't mind me sharing with you ... This past Thanksgiving I noticed that my brother was not his normal self. I really didn't have time to sit and talk with him. I decided that I would go visit him for a few day's and see what was going on in his life. When I got there he surprised me with an early Christmas gift, he was taking me out for dinner then to see your brother in concert. I was really excited about this, I mean my brother would never go to church with me when he was home, to have him actually sit next to me during this show was a miracle in it self!

During the show the love of God spilled out of Mark and unto everyone in the audience. I silently prayed during the night that my brother's heart would receive the love of Jesus. My Brother began to cry and in fact he jumped up and left the concert. I Followed him outside to his car, and it was there that he told me that he was about to embark on a lifestyle that would have changed his life forever! To make a long story short, He accepted Jesus into his heart right there in that parking lot !

I didn't get to meet Mark or "Lord Song" that night,

but I got my brother back! And that is the greatest Christmas gift I could have ever received! It's kind of funny and wonderful how God weaves people into our lives, I mean I know God has a reason for all things. Some people come into our lives for just a brief time and others for a lifetime. I often wondered why God placed you on my heart so many times. Your story of baby "Will" truly touched my heart and then I rejoiced with you when the Lord blessed you with Baby Katelyn!

I thank God the day your Mom came to my hometown, I thank God I heard your story, I thank God your brother was there for my brother. I sent out a package today to you and your family and one gift for Mark, it's a frame and a little saying on it about being a fishermen for the Lord . (He caught a big fish for God the other night! lol) I Don't really consider it just a gift from me, but from all the faces out there who are deeply touched by such a wonderful guy with such a strong meaningful message.

I think what you and your family do for others is such an awesome blessing to us all .... Thank you all, for what you do.

God bless you,
Chrissy

+++++++++++++

(10) Mark's Email to Mrs. Hollan's E-mail on March 17, 2005
From: Mark Lowry
Date: Thu, 17 Mar 2005 11:48:32 AM

Hi Mrs. Hollan!

It was great to hear from you. I'm going to forward your email to my mom and dad. They ask about you nearly every time I see them, believe it or not. They really do appreciate you and so do I.

I'm going to have Bob (my office manager) send you one of everything we have. You shouldn't have to buy ANYTHING of mine.

Please send me your mailing address and he'll get it all right out to you!
Thanks,
Mark

++++++++++++++

(11) An E-mail To Mark from Mrs. Roman Hollan (Mark's third grade teacher)
To: Mark Lowry
March 17, 2005 8:33:19 PM CST
(**Side Note**: This date is the 27th year anniversary of Mark's near fatal accident just five miles south of Carlisle, Pennsylvania on **March 17, 1978**)

Hi again!

Am I ever impressed! I was hoping that E-mail didn't even get through as I'm sure there were many errors in it. I usually think faster than I type, so many times it comes out all wrong. I know you do the same thing!

You really don't have to send me everything you have made, but I can tell you that I have loaned the videos that I have out to many youth groups, etc. here in Hempstead that they're almost worn out! Our pastor is a former undercover policeman for the Houston Police Dept. and has a heart for the young folks. When he found out I taught you, he had a video in which you mention my name and some way he showed part of it and brought up the fact that no matter where God plants us He can always use us. Since then I hear quite often..."Oh, you taught Mark Lowry". We probably did something illegal, but we made transparencies of your book, "Mary Did You Know" and flashed it on the screen as my son, daughter-in-law, and daughter sang your song. I'm sure it helped you to sell lots of copies. Did I do wrong?? Do I owe you royalties??? Keep up the good work. I won't bug you again, except to tell you that I did buy a book several years ago, "14,000 Quips & Quotes" for Writers and Speakers. I haven't gotten it mailed (just a little slow in my young-old age!) Thought you might use some new lines!! If you think you might be able to use it, let me know.

Keep working for the Lord 'til He comes! God bless you.
Mrs. Ramona Hollan

++++++++++++++

(12) Dear Ms Lowry, I do so look forward to meeting you at Marks Senior Class Trip in April. I was wondering if you can give me any advice in dealing with someone who I believe is hyperactive. The doctors don't see it because when she is there it is for only a few minutes and she is usually really good for those few minutes. I am talking about my 2 granddaughters. The 4 year old is very hyperactive and most of the time when she is doing something, if you try to talk to her, she acts like she doesn't even hear you. If she gets chocolate or too much sugar, she bounces off the wall. We cut her off from that. But when she gets overly excited, it is very hard, if not impossible, to get her under control. She does things that are destructive a lot too. But she can be just the sweetest child too, and very loving. The 6 year old I don't think is hyperactive, but she has a severe anger problem. We don't know what to do with her. We have tried so many things, and she can be good for a day at the most, but then the anger takes over. The anger didn't start until her daddy started to build their house.

Unfortunately he doesn't see his family too much because he is holding down a full time job and trying to build his house too. But that is the only way they can afford to build. We tried to get help from our church, but no one ever showed up or called when we asked. Bev, they live here with my husband and myself and I am at a loss as to what to do. It is causing so much stress for me seeing what is going on. The girls both attend a Christian school with one in first grade and the other in pre-K. The teachers don't see any of the things that I have described, except the reaction to chocolate and sugar for the 4 year old. I would appreciate any advice you can give me. I don't know where else to turn. I've tried seeking help from godly women in the church and the pastor, but didn't get much help. Thank you so much.

Carla
11-Jan-2006 19:13:13

+++++++++++++

(13) Dear Beverly,

Our pastors, Danny & Pam Wendt, of First Baptist Church, just returned from Mark's Senior Trip. They were just bubbling with excitement. The trip was a gift from our congregation for five years of dedicated service. They said the trip was awesome, fabulous, and loads of fun! I'm so proud of my former third grade student. Thanks for being the kind of mother you always were—always supportive, kind, sweet and in touch with God. Love and Prayers,
Ramona Hollan
10-Apr-2006 07:43:28

+++++++++++++

(14) I recently heard you at my church in Chattanooga, Tennessee (Calvary Baptist)... You were truly a blessing to my heart! Thank you for finding Mark's niche and training him to use his talent for Jesus...he has been a blessing to our family...especially my eight year old .."A merry heart doeth good like a medicine."
Jennifer
17-May-2006 16:32:44

+++++++++++++

(15) My daughter and I enjoyed listening to your interview on Mark's radio show. She was blessed & encouraged when you said that the same traits for ADHD were found in the definition for giftedness. She says it's nice to hear something positive instead of the negative about ADHD.

Sincerely,
Carol
09-Jun-2005 22:03:10

+++++++++++++

(16) JUST LOVE YOUR FAMILY, GOD HAS REALLY BLESSED YOU WITH A WONDERFUL SON MARK, MY GRANDSON BAILEY WANTS

TO BE JUST LIKE MARK. HE IS ADHD, 9 YEARS OLD, AND GOES AROUND PULLING HIS PANTS UP TO HIS CHIN. WE ALL LAUGH AT HIM AS WE DO MARK. HE LOVES MARK SO MUCH. LOVED THE PICTURES OF MISSY'S BABY. SHE IS SO CUTE. BEV YOU ARE BLESSED.

JANICE
29-Jun-2005 11:29:44

"Hyperactivity" and ADD and ADHD References
Ritalin Resources (and its dangers)

(1) http://ritalindeath.com

+++++++++++++

Title: ADHD and Giftedness: What Do We Really Know? and other ADD/ADHD resources at:

Family Education.com

Description: Get the latest on what the top experts know about ADHD and Giftedness in our children.

(1) http://school.familyeducation.com

(2) http://school.familyeducation.com/learning-disabilities/add-and-adhd/34474.html

(3) http://school.familyeducation.com/parents-and-school/parents-and-teacher/38636.html?mail-06-12

(4) http://school.familyeducation.com/special-education/education-and-state/34580.html?mail-06-12

(5) http://school.familyeducation.com/learningdisabilities/treatments/37763.html?mail-06-12

(6) http://school.familyeducation.com/learning-disabilities/treatments/37763.html?relinks&mail-05-27

(7) http://school.familyeducation.com/add-and-adhd/gifted-education/42644.html

(8) http://school.familyeducation.com/gifted-education/early-learning/55582.html

(9) http://quizzes.family education.com/learning-disabilities/school-psychology/55593.html

+++++++++++++

(1) http://life.familyeducation.com/add-and-adhd/medications/40435.html?mail-06-12

(2) http://life.familyeducation.com/add-and-adhd/medications/42243.html?mail-06-12

(3) http://life.familyeducation.com/gifted-education/school/41323.html?mail-06-12

+++++++++++++

(1) http://borntoexplore.org/gifted.html
(2) http://www.hoagiesgifted.org/

+++++++++++++

(1) www.3StepsADD.com

NOTE: I want to say one more thing:

I really don't believe in Hyperactivity anymore. It is Creativity. The characteristics are the same for both. Find your child's creativity niche. It may be singing, painting, sports or many other things. Find their niche and push them into doing that. Be careful with medication.

Pray, pray, pray and God Bless you. If you have any questions, email me: ruhyper@gmail.com

Love you and I am praying for all of you.

Bev Lowry

PS: You may also go to my website:

http://www.bevlowry.com

The Last Word!

Mark has said "Mama always wanted the last word." Now he gets it.

This article, written by Mark Lowry, first appeared in *Guideposts* magazine.

I was hyperactive, had a short attention span and acted on impulse. I thought I would never amount to anything.

When I was a kid, my hyperactivity was always getting me into trouble. Most people figured I would grow up to be a criminal. A little voice inside me convinced me I was a failure, that I would never amount to anything. I had what's known today as A.D.D. (Attention Deficit Disorder). Back then, they called it B.R.A.T. But, I wasn't your normal brat. I was so off-the-wall that I had air bags on my baby buggy. I was seven years old before I knew my name wasn't 'Settle Down'. At school, I tried to behave and be like the other kids but I had a short attention span and was in perpetual motion. Things popped into my brain that I had no control over, like, 'Get up and run around the room'. Something brilliant was always escaping my mouth before I could stop it.

When I was in the third grade, I had a teacher who understood kids like me. Mrs. Hollan an older lady with big fluffy hands; she loved children. When I couldn't sit still, she'd ask the student teacher to take over the class. We would go for a walk around the Hollibrook Elementary School and she would tell me, "Mark, it's okay to be hyperactive. God likes hyperactive kids."

Now, I had heard people say God loved me, before, but I had never heard anybody say God liked me. Knowing that helped because I had a big self-image problem. Other kids made fun of me because I had a little bitty body and a huge head. When I wore a ball cap, it looked like a thimble sitting on a grapefruit. And I never was any good at sports. Besides the fact that I was about as coordinated as a blob of Silly Putty, I had a hard time staying still long enough for a ball to get to me. When I went out for baseball, they made me the water boy.

For most of my childhood, I was on Ritalin. I could have been the poster boy for hyperactivity. Every day, I came home from school with notes hanging on my lapel, from teachers, telling about all the messes I had managed to get myself into. But, at night, Mama and Daddy always tucked me into bed and reassured me: "There are not enough trees and there's not enough paper for us to stop loving you. And, God is even better than that. One day, God's going to use you, Mark, but until he does, take this pill."

By the grace of God, I managed to get through high school. In 1976, I went away to college to study business and, during that time, I felt God was calling me into the music ministry. Nobody was more surprised than I was because I couldn't read music.

I began singing with the college evangelistic team. However, an encounter between our van and an 18-wheeler one night, on the way home from a church concert, was the end of that. I thought my ministry was over but a friend decided he would be my booking agent. This guy was amazing. He called churches where they didn't know him and didn't know me. And, next thing I knew, I was booked for 43 concerts in 41 days. I set out on the road with my clothes on a rod across the back seat of my car and a sound system in my trunk.

When I sang in churches, I got antsy while soundtracks were being changed. Those few seconds seemed like an eternity. To pass the time and lighten things up, I found myself telling stories about my life - my hyperactive childhood, my visits with a psychiatrist as a third grader and my older brother, who was so perfect we used his halo for a night-light.

Something began to happen. People laughed at my monologues. At first, I thought they were laughing at my testimony, but, then I figured it out. Here would come Mr. Serious in a polyester suit and vest singing a soft, slow song that practically put an audience into a coma. Who expected humor to be coming next? Soon, my singing was just an act that I used to lull folks before I zinged 'em.

For eight years, I traveled around the country and slept on pastors' couches, ate in their homes, schmoozed the congregations and got nowhere. The road got to be a real downer. I remember one gig, in particular. I had sung every song I knew, told all my stories and did the best I could. After the applause died down, the pastor walked up to me, stuck out his hand, gave me a big old smile and said, "Thank you for coming." Then, he just walked away. That was it. No love offering, not even ten bucks for gas money.

I was tired and hungry and, deep down inside, I was ticked. Not at the church folks - I was mad at God. I drove down the Pennsylvania Turnpike and, for a solid hour, I told God exactly what I thought. "Your employee didn't get paid tonight," I reminded Him, "My stomach likes food. This car likes gas. We'll be hitching rides in a matter of days. What are we going to do?"

Every year, I went to Estes Park, Colorado, for the Christian Artists Seminar in the Rockies. During the day, I took songwriting courses and entered competitions with other aspiring artists. At night, we saw acts featuring established performers. As I watched from back in the registrant area, I thought, "I can't sing as good as any of them but I can sure talk as good as any of them. If I could just get up there on stage, I know I could say something everybody could relate to."

Then, in 1988, while I was in Los Angeles to perform at some churches, I had dinner with my good friend, Lynn Barrington. Lynn really knows the record industry and I'd always found her to be a straightforward, objective person. We cornered ourselves off at a quiet table at the Moustache Cafe."I just don't understand it," I confided, as I polished off a chocolate souffle. "I'm doing two hundred concerts a year. People like my stories. I've gone to Estes Park for eight years in a row but I can't get a record company even to look at me."

Lynn didn't mince words. "The people at Estes Park aren't your source, Mark, God is. All your bills are being paid and you've never missed a meal - obviously. You've never had to work Monday through Friday so you could go out and sing on the weekends. You know what your problem is? You're ungrateful. Why should God give you any more when you haven't even stopped to thank Him for what you've already got?"

I gulped. She was right. I didn't have to be somewhere Monday morning asking, "You want fries with that?" God had taken a hyperactive kid who most folks thought would be locked up by then and given him all these opportunities. I hadn't even thought to thank Him. As soon as I was alone, I prayed: "From day one, you've taken care of me God. Please forgive me."

Once I began to appreciate my blessings, my whole outlook changed. In fact, I grew so content that, when a door finally opened at Estes Park six months later, I almost didn't walk through it. I was having a blast working with kids at a camp at Jekyll Island, Georgia, when the call came offering me a spot on the program. I couldn't see flying all the way to Colorado, performing for ten minutes and, then, flying right back to camp. But, friends kept the phone lines hot, "You've just got to do this," they pressed.

When I got there, Sandi Patty was hosting the program. When Sandi sings, sometimes my goosebumps get goosebumps. All of a sudden, she introduced me and I was scared out of my mind. I took the mic and immediately started hyperventilating, praying and talking. (I can do three things at once; it's one of the benefits of being hyperactive.) "If Sandi laughs, I'll do anything you want me to do God. I'll go to Africa. I'll wear polyester Bermuda shorts for the rest of my life..."

"I grew up in a strict church home," I began, "and, ever since, I've wanted to do a church my way. I'm putting in La-Z-Boys with Big Gulp holders and a remote control. I figure, if you're going to sleep, you might as well enjoy it."

Everyone howled and I was on a roll. "When the church doors were open," I continued, "the Lowry family was all right there. But, don't think I didn't try to get out of going - like any normal kid. Many times, I'd say 'Daddy, I'm too sick to go to church'. He'd say, 'Throw up and prove it'. If I couldn't throw up, I went to church. And, if I did throw up, he'd say, 'Now, don't you feel better? Let's go to church'."

When I' looked out into the audience, Sandi Patty was leaned over - laughing. All those years, I had looked up to her and, now, I was making this dear, gifted person laugh. Thank you, God. Thank You.

As I left that exhilarating standing ovation behind to go back to camp, at last I understood. God had designed me a little differently to fill the place in his plan reserved just for me. My hyperactivity, short attention span and impulsiveness weren't defects at all. Rather, they were God's gifts in disguise. When I turned them over to Him, He channeled them into a package of skills just perfect for a comedian: high energy, enthusiasm, creativity, spontaneity, the ability to read an audience quickly. It's like that verse in the Bible says: "My grace is sufficient for you, for my power is made perfect in weakness." (II Corinthians 12:9, NIV).

Mama and Daddy were right. God was going to use me. And, wherever that might be, I would do it joyfully.

These days, through the use of humor, I try to get people to take God more seriously and themselves less seriously. For I believe, with all my heart, that when God hears His children's laughter, He smiles.